PORTUGUESE STUDIES

Volume 35 Number 1
2019

Founding Editor
Helder Macedo

Editors
Catarina Fouto
Tori Holmes
Paulo de Medeiros
Paul Melo e Castro
Hilary Owen
Claire Williams

Editorial Assistant
Richard Correll

Production Editor
Graham Nelson

MODERN HUMANITIES RESEARCH ASSOCIATION

PORTUGUESE STUDIES

A peer-reviewed biannual multi-disciplinary journal devoted to research on the cultures, literatures, history and societies of the Lusophone world

International Advisory Board

David Brookshaw   Maria Manuel Lisboa
João de Pina Cabral   Kenneth Maxwell
Ivo José de Castro   Laura de Mello e Souza
Thomas F. Earle   Maria Irene Ramalho
John Gledson   Silviano Santiago
Anna Klobucka

Portuguese Studies and other journals published by the MHRA may be ordered from Turpin Distribution (http://ebiz.turpin-distribution.com/).

The **Modern Humanities Research Association** was founded in Cambridge in 1918 and has become an international organization with members in all parts of the world. It is a registered charity number 1064670, and a company limited by guarantee, registered in England number 3446016. Its main object is to encourage advanced study and research in modern and medieval European languages, literatures, and cultures by its publication of journals, book series, and its Style Guide. Further information about the activities of the Association and individual membership may be obtained from the Membership Secretary, email membership@mhra.org.uk, or from the website at: **www.mhra.org.uk**

Disclaimer: Statements of fact and opinion in the content of *Portuguese Studies* are those of the respective authors and contributors and not of the journal editors or of the Modern Humanities Research Association (MHRA). MHRA makes no representation, express or implied, in respect of the accuracy of the material in this journal and cannot accept any legal responsibility or liability for any errors or omissions that may be made.

Parts of this work may be reproduced as permitted under legal provisions for fair dealing (or fair use) for the purposes of research, private study, criticism, or review, or when a relevant collective licensing agreement is in place. All other reproduction requires the written permission of the copyright holder who may be contacted at rights@mhra.org.uk.

ISSN 0267-5315 (print) ISSN 2222-4270 (online)
ISBN 978-1-78188-888-9

© 2019 The Modern Humanities Research Association
Salisbury House, Station Road, Cambridge CB1 2LA, United Kingdom

Portuguese Studies Vol. 35 No. 1

CONTENTS

Irony in the *Peregrinação* THOMAS EARLE	5
Geographical Knowledge and Mineral Riches in the Struggle for Sovereignty and Possession of Southern Brazil (1750–1755) DENISE MOURA	20
Transnational Perspectives in Early Twentieth-Century Portugal: The Emergence of the Periodical *Sociedade Futura* (Lisbon, 1902–1904) CHRISTINA BEZARI	39
Hybridity and Prejudice: Jews and New Christians in *Casa-Grande & Senzala* and the Intellectual Context of Gilberto Freyre CLAUDE B. STUCZYNSKI	55
Pessoa, Unknown to Paz JERÓNIMO PIZARRO	77
Fragmenting Colonial Stereotypes in the Films *Chocolat* (1988) and *Tabu* (2012) SANDRA RELLIER	90
Reviews	105
Abstracts	119

NOTES FOR CONTRIBUTORS

Articles to be considered for publication may be on any subject within the field but must not exceed 7,500 words, and should be submitted in a form ready for publication in English, sent as an email attachment to the Editorial Assistant at portuguese@mhra.org.uk.

Contributions whose standard of English is inadequate will be returned. Any quotations in Portuguese must be accompanied by an English translation. Submissions in Portuguese may be considered, but full peer review and publication will be conditional on provision of a satisfactory translation by or on behalf of the author. The Editorial Assistant may undertake translations on request for a reasonable charge.

Text and references should conform precisely to the conventions of the *MHRA Style Guide*, 3rd edn, 2013 (978-1-78188-009-8), £9.50, $19.00, €12.00, obtainable in print or online version from www.style.mhra.org.uk. All articles are subject to independent, anonymous peer review by experts in the field; authors receive written feedback on the editors' decision and guidance on any revisions required. *Portuguese Studies* regrets it must charge contributors for the cost of corrections in proof deemed excessive.

It is a condition of publication in this journal that authors of articles and reviews assign copyright, including electronic copyright, to the MHRA. Inter alia, this allows the General Editor to deal efficiently and consistently with requests from third parties for permission to reproduce material. The journal has been published simultaneously in printed and electronic form since January 2001. Permission, without fee, for authors to use their own material in other publications, after a reasonable period of time has elapsed, is not normally withheld. Authors may make closed-access deposit of accepted manuscripts in their academic institution's digital repository upon acceptance. Full open access to the accepted manuscript is permitted no sooner than 12 months following publication of the Contribution by the MHRA. Contributions may also be republished on authors' personal websites without seeking further permission from the Association, but no earlier than 12 months after publication by the MHRA.

Books for review should be sent to: Reviews Editor, *Portuguese Studies*, Dr Paul Melo e Castro, School of Modern Languages and Cultures, 221b, Hetherington Building, University of Glasgow, Bute Gardens, Glasgow G12 8RS.

Irony in the *Peregrinação*[1]

Thomas Earle

University of Oxford

The history of the criticism of the *Peregrinação* is a long one, for Mendes Pinto has never been one of those forgotten authors of whom there are so many in Portugal. Yet the critical tradition has not always been satisfying intellectually, largely due to the tendency to judge the *Peregrinação* by standards extraneous to the text, for example, its truth to historical fact or its adherence, or otherwise, to the ideology of a Christian empire. After a review of this tradition an attempt will be made to understand the *Peregrinação* on its own terms, as a work of literature, through Mendes Pinto's rhetoric of irony, verbal but above all situational. Irony turns out to be a consistent way of approaching the book, both in terms of its overall structure but also at the level of the detail of the numerous micro-narratives which it contains. In the end irony itself seems to be ironized, for if on the one hand Mendes Pinto's world is one of constant flux and confusion, on the other he never abandons his faith in an all-powerful, if incomprehensible, Providence.

The notion that the *Peregrinação* might be an ironical work is not new, and can be found, along with many other concerns, in the work of one of Pinto's earliest critics, and his first translator, the Spanish cleric Francisco de Herrera Maldonado, whose *Historia oriental de las peregrinaciones de Fernan Mendez Pinto* of 1620 appeared only six years after the original. Since Herrera Maldonado lived close in time to Pinto, who died around 1578, his concerns, and also his apparent omissions, deserve attention.

Herrera Maldonado prefaced his translation with an extremely lengthy 'Apología en favor de Fernan Mendez Pinto' in which he started the debate, far from exhausted even today, about the truthfulness of the experiences narrated in the *Peregrinação*. Herrera Maldonado was convinced of the book's factual accuracy, and went to great pains to prove it, by listing an immense number of other works that seemed to him to corroborate what Pinto had said. The French and English translators of the book reproduced much of Herrera Maldonado's researches, but they failed to convince all their readers and, as is well known, Pinto became a byword for mendacity in England from as early as

---

[1] This article is a much expanded and revised version of a paper read at a conference on the *Peregrinação* organized by Zoltán Biedermann and Catarina Fouto and held in London in December 2014. I have particularly valued the comments and suggestions made during the conference and after it by Zoltán Biedermann and Joan-Pau Rubiés.

the seventeenth century.[2] His reputation reached its lowest point around 1900, when the Scottish researcher Donald Ferguson and, later, the German Jesuit Georg Schurhammer, rejected much of what he wrote as fantasy.[3]

As will appear shortly, opinion has changed, and more recent writers have rehabilitated the *Peregrinação*. Back in 1620, Herrera Maldonado's prime concern was to prove that Pinto was not a liar. However, that is not all that he says about the *Peregrinação*. In some respects he was unsympathetic to the text whose historical value he praised so highly, for he considered it to have been very badly written. That opinion led him to take great liberties as a translator, a point which I will return to later. Yet, despite Pinto's deficiencies as a stylist, his book is truly worth reading, says the critic, because of its almost infinite variety. Any reader can find in it something to enjoy.

Hidden within Herrera Maldonado's words is a point which has informed much later criticism. According to him, Pinto gives the reader many lessons about life, and also consolation for its ups and downs, in a way which is often antithetical. So there is the comic, 'cosas de riso', and the serious, 'el grave'. There is something for the thoughtful, 'los doctos', 'el discreto', but also for the emotional man, 'el melancólico', 'el más triste', 'el desdichado', while at the end of the passage the miser is contrasted with the warrior.[4] Herrera Maldonado does not employ the word irony here, for that term was not used in the early modern period for the situational ironies which modern readers find so easily in the *Peregrinação*. Yet it seems as though he recognized their presence, in the constant oppositions to which his critical commentary makes reference.

Bernard Figuier's French translation includes critical material which mostly derives from Herrera Maldonado, as already mentioned. However, in the final paragraph of his 'Deffence apologeticque' he brings into sharper focus Pinto's fascination with contraries, particularly the opposition between good fortune and bad, which he calls 'les idées des biens ou des maux, des contentements ou des douleurs, des prosperitez ou des infortunes'. It is a point which has struck many readers over the centuries.

It was around these points, then, especially the question of Pinto's veracity, that the early modern debate about him revolved. In the nineteenth century José Feliciano de Castilho brought some additional ideas to the text, and these have also continued to reverberate ever since. By the 1840s, when Castilho was

---

[2] In modern times the comments by Congreve and Dorothy Osborne about Pinto's lies were uncovered by Charles Boxer, who passed on the information to Maurice Collis. See Maurice Collis, *The Grand Peregrination* (Manchester: Carcanet, 1990), p. 298. Collis's book was first published in 1949. For the French and English translations, see the 'Deffence apologeticque' included by Bernard Figuier in his *Les voyages adventureux de Fernand Mendez Pinto* (Paris: Mathurin Henault, 1628) and 'An Apologetical Defence of Fernan Mendez Pinto His History' in Henry Cogan's *The Voyages and Adventures of Fernan Mendez Pinto* (London: Henry Cripps and Lodowick Lloyd, 1653).
[3] Donald Ferguson, *Letters from Portuguese Captives in Ceylon, Written in 1534 and 1536* (Bombay: Education Society, 1902) and Georg Schurhammer, *Franz Xaver, sein Leben und seine Zeit* (Freiburg: Herder, 1955).
[4] I have consulted the edition of 1645 (Valencia, Bernardo Noguer).

writing, it was known that Pinto had been accepted into the Society of Jesus, as a lay brother, and that in that capacity he had written two letters about his experiences in the East. Scholars were also aware that he had later abandoned the order and returned to secular life. Castilho believed that, in revenge, the Jesuits interfered with the text of the *Peregrinação* over the long period, of more than thirty years, that elapsed between the completion of the manuscript and its publication.[5] In this way there began to emerge the theory that in some ways Pinto was a religious sceptic or, at any rate, that his statements of commitment to Christianity were not his own, but added by a Jesuitical censor. In the next century Rodrigues Lapa, for instance, cast doubt on the authenticity of the long section (chs 203–15) describing the activities of Francis Xavier in the East.[6] As will appear later, however, it is possible to read these chapters and the rest of the *Peregrinação* in a way that is internally consistent.

Near the start of his study of Pinto, Castilho says, without taking full responsibility for his words, that some readers think that the *Peregrinação* is an allegorical novel, based on Pinto's experiences in the East, critical of the excesses which the Portuguese committed there.[7] However, much of what he says about Pinto follows traditional lines. For the most part, Castilho, like Herrera Maldonado before him, believed that Pinto was a truthful, informative and entertaining writer. However, along with his remarks about the Jesuits (to whom he gave considerable space) and the statement that the book is an allegorical novel he gave publicity to a vision of the *Peregrinação* which was very different from the traditional one. Pinto now becomes, not a faithful chronicler of events, but a creative and subversive literary artist whose book contains concealed meanings, hidden from the ecclesiastical censor, but accessible to those with the appropriate understanding. What is more, critics who believe that the book was subject to clerical interference before publication can reject as spurious anything in the book with which they do not agree, most obviously, statements of religious orthodoxy.

Here is a cluster of approaches to Pinto that were taken up with enthusiasm by a number of influential critics of the mid- to late twentieth century. One of the first of these was Rodrigues Lapa, whose anthology of the *Peregrinação*, first published in 1946, was many times reprinted. In the introduction, as already noted, doubt is cast on the authenticity of Pinto's account of Francis Xavier's missionary activities. Lapa interprets Pinto's Portuguese adventurers as occasionally heroic, but invariably also venal and piratical, and the unfavourable comments made about their behaviour by Asian characters are expressions of

---

[5] See Fernão Mendes Pinto, *Excertos, seguidos de uma notícia sobre sua vida e obras, um juízo crítico, apreciações de belezas e defeitos, e estudos da língua*, ed. by José Feliciano de Castilho, 2 vols (Rio de Janeiro: Garnier, 1865), II, 214–16 and 276–77. Castilho dates his book to 1845, twenty years before its publication, II, 288.
[6] Fernão Mendes Pinto, *Peregrinação*, ed. by Rodrigues Lapa (Lisbon: Textos Literários, 1946), p. xiv.
[7] Castilho, II, 163.

the outrage which anyone, Asian or European, might feel. According to Lapa, the words of oriental speakers can, at least sometimes, be read allegorically, so that, for example, when a priest from Pegu (now part of Myanmar) delivers a sermon condemning tyranny in his own country (ch. 168), he should be understood as referring to European monarchs and perhaps even to Portugal itself. The selection of texts which follows Lapa's introduction is chosen to support his view of the book as a whole, and generations of university students in the UK, for example, have read the episode of the Ilha dos Ladrões and the Chinese boy (chs 53–55) as a condemnation of Portuguese activities in Asia.

This famous story will be mentioned several times in the course of this essay. Most critics focus on one section of it only, though it continues over three chapters. They seize on the moment when a boy, found on board a Chinese ship which the Portuguese have stolen, rebukes his capturers for their hypocrisy in words which are a stunning rebuke:

'Sabeis porque vo-lo digo? Porque vos vi louvar a Deus depois de fartos, com as mãos alevantadas e com os beiços untados, como homens a quem parece que basta arreganhar os dentes ao céu sem satisfazer o que têm roubado.'[8]

It is undoubtedly a striking moment in Pinto's narrative, although, as will appear over the course of this article, it is possible to draw more than one conclusion from it.

Lapa's ideas were developed further in the 1950s and early 1960s by António José Saraiva — to whose work Lapa refers favourably in later editions of his anthology — and, in the 1970s, by Rebecca Catz, whose English version may be the first of the complete text. Earlier translators were inclined to make selections, while Maurice Collis's well-known *The Grand Peregrination* is explicitly a narrative based on the text of Pinto's book, and not a complete translation. Catz includes studies which seek to interpret the book as a whole, on broadly the same lines as Saraiva's essay, which had been published not many years previously. Both critics reflected the political climate of the years of the end of the colonial empires and the diminution of European influence in the East, and both have been very influential.

The premise which both take as their point of departure is that the *Peregrinação* is a work of literature. It may contain autobiographical or other factual material, but that material is organized in such a way as to produce a consistent effect on the reader. Both critics agree that the literary technique

---

[8] 'Do you know why I am speaking to you in this way? Because I saw you praise God with full bellies, with your hands raised [in prayer] and greasy lips, like men for whom it is enough to bare their teeth to heaven without restoring what they have stolen' [my translation here and throughout]. Fernão Mendes Pinto, *Peregrinação*, ed. by Maria Alberta Menéres, 2 vols (Lisbon: Relógio d'Água, 2001), ch. 55; I, 173. This modernized edition is the only one known to me which presents a readable version of Pinto's work. However, the editor sometimes takes undue liberties with the text which are here silently corrected by reference to the first edition of 1614. Further references to Menéres's edition will be given after quotations in the text.

employed by Pinto is satirical, and that the target of his satire is the Portuguese presence in the East and the ideology, imperial and religious, which justified that presence.

However, what Catz and Saraiva say is not exactly the same. Saraiva tried to relate the *Peregrinação* to the Iberian, more specifically Spanish, *pícaro* tradition, whereby the narrator becomes an underdog, commenting cynically on the antics of his social superiors.[9] Catz has a broader view of satire, and claims that at any time the narrator will adopt one of three postures from which to observe, and criticize the world around him.[10] However, Pinto is for both the outsider, detached from the European empire-building project, and more sympathetic to some of the Asians that he meets than to his fellow countrymen and co-religionists.

These critics of the late twentieth century certainly deserve praise for taking the *Peregrinação* seriously, and for trying to understand it as a whole. However, their approach contains many inconsistencies, some of them at least partly recognized by Lapa, Saraiva and Catz themselves, the most obvious of which is that Pinto himself appears so often to be inconsistent. So, after a passage in which he claims that Pinto satirizes all religions, Catholicism included, Saraiva observes that there are moments when Pinto reveals himself to be a pious and orthodox Catholic.[11] The resolution of the contradiction is to fall back on censorship and the Inquisition, but that is to rely on unprovable assertions about the nature and extent of ecclesiastical interference in Pinto's text before publication.

Back in 1946 Lapa had lamented that Pinto's narratives are so often unfinished — one might say, always unfinished — claiming that he was a writer who speaks more to the reader's feelings than to his intellect.[12] Here perhaps is another admission of critical failure, because the implication of Lapa's comment is that Pinto is not in control of his material. That might be true, but it would then be impossible for the book to be read as a consistent criticism of the Portuguese in Asia. Thirty years later Rebecca Catz had still not solved the problem.

Distinguishing between what is intended to be satirical and what is not, in a book as long and as diverse as this one, is extremely difficult. Where does one fragment end and another begin? Saraiva himself explains how, for many chapters, Pinto himself almost disappears from the narrative, which becomes instead the history, or histories, of the modern countries of Myanmar and Thailand, and the island of Java in what is now Indonesia.[13] While his praise of the perfections of China has been understood as an indirect attack on the imperfections of sixteenth-century Portuguese society, no one has seen Pinto's

---

[9] António José Saraiva, 'Fernão Mendes Pinto, ou a sátira picaresca da ideologia senhorial', in *História da Cultura em Portugal*, 3 vols (Lisbon: Jornal do Foro, 1962), III, 343–496 (pp. 396–417).
[10] Rebecca Catz, *A sátira social de Fernão Mendes Pinto* (Lisbon: Prelo, 1978), pp. 95–118.
[11] Saraiva, p. 482.
[12] *Fernão Mendes Pinto*, ed. by Lapa, p. xviii.
[13] Saraiva, p. 371.

narratives of the wars of the Burmese and Siamese monarchs as having critical or satirical meanings of that kind, even if Lapa did try to get some mileage out of a sermon preached in Myanmar, as mentioned above. It has, however, been possible for the modern historians of the countries involved to use the *Peregrinação* as a broadly accurate account of public events during the time that Pinto was in South-East Asia.[14] It is very difficult to read any of these sections of the *Peregrinação* as satirical, though insofar as they chart the ups and downs of political and military affairs they may still be regarded as ironical.

Trying to see the *Peregrinação* as a satirical work, therefore, runs the risk of internal contradiction. The claim that Pinto was essentially anti-Catholic is also difficult to sustain, particularly when made by critics who believe that his book was subject to ecclesiastical censorship before publication. Saraiva and Catz would then have to explain why the censors missed so much, but they never do so.

Herrera Maldonado, Pinto's first translator and critic, was a cleric himself, but never appears to question the orthodoxy of the *Peregrinação*, though it appears to contain many surprising and challenging statements about religion. That he should not interfere with them is particularly telling, because in most other respects Herrera Maldonado was an extremely unfaithful translator. He felt that it was his duty to improve on Pinto, who was, in his view, an uncultivated writer. So he expands what is already a long book, adding to it the rhetorical 'artificio' that he believed was lacking. The Chinese boy — to take one example among many — is just as condemnatory in Spanish as he is in Portuguese; it is just that he speaks at greater length, as these extracts will show, taken from the point in the story when the boy has been suddenly converted to Christianity by his captor, the Portuguese commander António de Faria. The unexpectedly eloquent neophyte speaks as follows:

> Pinto: 'Bendita seja, Senhor, a tua paciência, que sofre haver na terra gente que fale tão bem de ti e use tão pouco da tua lei.' (ch. 55; I, 173)[15]
>
> Herrera Maldonado: 'Bendita sea, gran señor, tu sagrada paciencia, pues sufres en la tierra gente que hable tan bien de ti, de tu ley, y de sus misterios, y de ellos, e de ella use tan mal, y a ti te sirva tan poco...'[16]

The rebuke may be more telling in its original, Portuguese version, but the Spanish translator makes no attempt to hide it.

The behaviour of the morally dubious António de Faria certainly merits criticism, though Pinto's choice of critic is unusual. Nor does Herrera

---

[14] For example, see the articles collected in *Fernão Mendes Pinto and the Peregrinação*, ed. by Jorge Santos Alves (Lisbon: Fundação Oriente, 2010), Maria da Conceição Flores, *Os portugueses e o Sião no século XVI* (Lisbon: Imprensa Nacional-Casa da Moeda, 1995), pp. 52, 58, 90–91, 104–06 etc., and Maria Ana Marques Guedes, *Interferência e integração dos portugueses na Birmânia* (Lisbon: Fundação Oriente, 1994), pp. 54–56, 244–45.

[15] 'Blessed be your patience, Lord, for allowing there to be people on this earth who speak so well of you yet pay scant regard to your commandments'.

[16] Herrera Maldonado, p. 96, col. B.

Maldonado experience any difficulty in translating — and expanding — an attack made against no less a person than Francis Xavier who, besides being a fellow Spaniard, was in the course of being made a saint when the translation was published. (Francis Xavier was beatified in 1619 and canonized in 1622.) While at the court of the king, or *daimyo*, of Bungo, Francis Xavier engages in a religious disputation with the local Buddhist priests, or bonzes, which he wins. As he leaves, arm in arm with king, they call down a curse on their monarch: '[...] e deziam publicamente e em altas vozes que fogo do céu viesse sobre el-rei, pois se enganava tão facilmente com um feiticeiro vadio, sem nome' (ch. 213; II, 762).[17] Herrera Maldonado simply adds more insulting epithets: '[...] que decían a voces, que fuego del cielo cayesse sobre el rey, que se dexaba engañar tan facilmente de un hechicero, alvenidizo, sin nombre, fama ni letras'.[18]

It is surely not by chance that these words come in a prominent position, at the end of a chapter which also marks the end of Xavier's mission to Japan, for in the next chapter he embarks for China and an early death. Yet Herrera Maldonado translates them without adding any comment. Perhaps he felt that none was necessary, because his readers would hardly be likely to take seriously the peevish utterances of the priests of a false religion, who had just been worsted in theological argument. To a reader more attuned than Maldonado to the deep structure of Pinto's narrative the words must seem much more disturbing for, coming where they do, they could be understood as a summing-up of the Jesuit mission to Japan, at least from a Japanese point of view. However, the question of point of view is an issue which I will return to later. For the moment it is enough to recognize that Pinto's seventeenth-century translator was not troubled by statements in the *Peregrinação* which appear to be hostile to the Christian faith and its practitioners. Put differently, he seems to have been confident of Pinto's orthodoxy.

So are some modern critics, and Saraiva and Catz have not had it all their own way. Thomas R. Hart, for example, notes how the *Peregrinação* begins and ends with a statement of thanks to the creator whose Providence has guided the writer through every manner of misfortune, and Joan-Pau Rubiés also claims that 'beyond all the previous moral questioning there was a final reconciliation of the writer with the code of his own society'.[19] To the beginning and end of the book it is possible to add other moments in which Pinto expresses an unqualified devotion to the Christian faith, as for example in the encounter with Inês de Leiria, a Chinese of mixed racial descent who maintained, in the heart of the Middle Kingdom, the religious beliefs she had learnt from her Portuguese father (ch. 91; I, 282–86).

[17] 'They declared in public, raising their voices, that fire from heaven should fall upon the king, who was so easily deceived by a nameless, wandering witch-doctor'.
[18] Herrera Maldonado, p. 454, col. B.
[19] Thomas R. Hart, '"Pleasant Harmless Lies": Fernão Mendes Pinto's *Peregrination*', *Boletim de Filologia*, 29 (1984), 221–30 (pp. 222 and 229) and Joan-Pau Rubiés, 'The Oriental Voices of Mendes Pinto', *Portuguese Studies*, 10 (1994), 24–43 (p. 41).

This overview of the secondary literature about the *Peregrinação* reveals how differently it has been understood over the centuries. The translators of the seventeenth century, who were also critics, found in it much information and much diversion, though they were conscious too of aesthetic issues, particularly the book's antithetical structure. In the nineteenth and twentieth centuries the book has become much more serious, and much more subversive, full of denunciations of Portuguese conduct in the East and even — though with necessary qualifications — of their religion. Though the arguments of Lapa, Saraiva and Catz are not sustainable over the whole of Pinto's book, it is impossible for the modern reader not to agree that there is a critical, perhaps a satirical side to at least some of the episodes.

The advances in literary criticism made over the last century should lead us to the discovery of a conceptual tool capable of unlocking the *Peregrinação*, of uncovering its inner workings, and of suggesting a means by which contradictory interpretations might be reconciled. One tool which seems promising is that of irony. It is a word which only fairly recently has come to be used in discussion of the text. Catz and Rubiés mention it, and there is a more systematic account in John Christian Laursen's article of 2003.

An initial distinction must be made between irony as the term was understood in the sixteenth century and the way it is used today. Irony, which is probably universal in speech and writing, was defined, as a figure of speech, by theorists of rhetoric in the Middle Ages and the Renaissance. Mendes Pinto is not likely to have known their writings at first hand, but since the theorists said the same sort of things about irony for several hundred years, it is likely that literary practitioners had absorbed the message.

The most normal interpretation of irony, repeated endlessly, was that it stated the opposite to the intended meaning, and that it was generally, though not necessarily, used for the attribution of praise or blame.[20] One of the most famous instances of Renaissance irony is Mark Antony's funeral oration in Shakespeare's *Julius Caesar*, in which the speaker repeatedly refers to Brutus, one of the conspirators responsible for Caesar's murder, as 'an honourable man'. The audience knows that the words of praise are really an accusation, because in his speech Mark Antony insists on Caesar's numerous acts of public virtue, now cut short by his death.[21]

Mark Antony's true meaning is obvious, for he is addressing the Roman people at large and cannot afford ambiguity, even if the words he uses are ironic. Rhetorical ironies of this kind, where the words of a speaker are contradicted, in this case by himself, are not common in the *Peregrinação*, perhaps because of Mendes Pinto's lack of literary training. When they do occur their meaning is not easy to discern, as successive statements seem to cancel each other out. A good example is the last paragraph, in which the author laments that he never

---

[20] See Dilwyn Knox, *Ironia: Medieval and Renaissance Ideas on Irony* (Leiden: Brill, 1989), pp. 9, 14.
[21] William Shakespeare, *Julius Caesar*, Act III, Scene 2, ll. 74–108.

received the reward that he expected from the king. There is evident verbal irony in the following lines:

> Como eu em todos os reis deste reino (que são a fonte limpa donde manam as satisfações, inda que às vezes por canos mais afeiçoados que arrezoados) enxerguei sempre um zelo santo e agradecido, e um desejo larguíssimo e grandioso, não somente para galardoar a quem os serve, mas também para fazer muitas mercês ainda a quem os não serve. (ch. 226; II, 813)[22]

But very quickly the irony is set aside, and the failings of the royal administration are attributed, not to the king, but to divine justice, which uses human injustice as its instrument in punishing sin. It is on this note that the paragraph, and the whole book, end.

It is not easy to accept this statement on its own terms. After so much service, and so much suffering, involving repeated imprisonment and enslavement, does the author really repose in the certainty of divine justice? It is tempting to look for a structural irony here, whereby the glib words about God's will are contrasted with the record of intense struggle which the rest of the book records, and are found inadequate.

Tempting, but in the end wrong, because, as we have seen, Mendes Pinto's statements about divine Providence, repeated throughout the book, are a stable point which is never undermined. Here is an example from an episode which leads directly to Mendes Pinto's first meeting with Francis Xavier, one of the crucial encounters of the whole enormous narrative.

> Mas como Deus Nosso Senhor, com seus ocultos juízos ordena todas as coisas suavemente por uns meios que nos embaraçam o entendimento, permitiu ele pela razão que ele só entende, que com a lua nova de Dezembro, que foi aos cinco dias do mês, sobreviesse uma tão grande tempestade [...]. (ch. 202; II, 701)[23]

The storm, apparently a disaster, leads to the arrival on the scene of Angiró, the Japanese convert who, under the name of Paulo de Santa Fé, greatly assisted Xavier in his first missionary journey to Japan and then, having incurred the enmity of the bonzes, was exiled from his native country and murdered by robbers in China, a sad end which Pinto mentions twice (chs 203 and 208; II, 705 and 729).

The workings of Providence are indeed incomprehensible, but that is because, as Pinto says, they operate according to a process known only to God. The seemingly bad, the storm, leads to the good, the conversion of Angiró and his missionary work in Japan, and then back to the bad, his exile and

---

[22] 'Since I have invariably found in all the kings of Portugal (who are the pure spring from which satisfaction flows, even if sometimes by channels more partial than just) a holy and grateful zeal, and a magnificently generous desire, not just to reward those who have served them, but also to do great honour to those who have not served them'.
[23] 'But since God Our Lord, reserving His judgement, ordains the smooth running of all things by means beyond our understanding, He permitted, for a reason which only He can comprehend, that with the December new moon, on the 5th of the month, there should arise so great a tempest [...]'.

ignominious death. What is more, the story of Paulo de Santa Fé is only one of a whole host of stories surrounding the Jesuit mission to Japan, itself subject to many reversals — including the death of Xavier — and seemingly without any clear-cut conclusion. At any rate Pinto, whose book was completed long before the expulsion of the Jesuits by the Tokungawa shoguns, mentions none. Pinto's vision of the world as a place ruled by God in ways which man cannot understand is a religious one, but he gives expression to it in a way which is capable of literary analysis, through narratives, like the one just mentioned, which are chains of self-contradicting ironies.

Narrative or situational irony is not the same as the verbal irony whose presence in the last paragraph of the *Peregrinação* was discussed above, and neither Pinto nor the literary theorists of his day would have known the term 'situational irony', which appears to date from the eighteenth century.[24] However, as the comments of Herrera Maldonado and Figuier, quoted above, show, there is no doubt that his early readers recognized the phenomenon.

John Christian Laursen made an important advance towards the understanding of Pinto's irony when he related it to the categories of irony developed by Wayne C. Booth in his *A Rhetoric of Irony* of 1974.[25] However, Pinto's irony does not belong to the category of 'unstable irony', as Laursen claims, but to that of '"Stable" –Covert-Infinite' ironies in Booth's taxonomy.[26]

Booth had no knowledge of Portuguese, as he rather disarmingly admits,[27] and it is hardly surprising that he should say nothing about the *Peregrinação*. Most of his examples are taken from fiction written long after Pinto's time. However, Pinto seems to fit his categorization very well. Pinto's ironies are 'covert' because they are intended to be reconstructed by the reader. Pinto never uses the words 'irónico' or 'ironia', and, as already noted, he rarely uses the verbal ironies classified as such by the theorists of the classical and Renaissance periods. They are 'infinite' because Pinto's world is 'an infinite series of ironies, every one undermined by further ironies'.[28] Some examples of these have already been given, and further ones will follow. Finally, they are stable because Pinto is not a twentieth-century writer like Beckett, and his world is not essentially absurd or meaningless. As Booth puts it:

> For such an ironist [i.e., one like Pinto] it is not so much the whole of existence that is absurd as it is mankind in the proud claim to know something about it. His works may in some respects resemble Beckett's: every proposition will be doubted as soon as uttered, then undercut by some other proposition that in turn will prove inadequate. The meanings are finally covert. But both the effort to understand and the particular

---

[24] D. C. Muecke, *The Compass of Irony* (London: Methuen, 1969), p. 46.
[25] John Christian Laursen, 'Irony and Toleration: Lessons for the Travels of Mendes Pinto', *Critical Review of International Social and Political Philosophy*, 6 (2003), 21–40 (p. 31).
[26] Wayne C. Booth, *A Rhetoric of Irony* (Chicago, IL: University of Chicago Press, 1975), p. 267.
[27] Ibid., p. 279.
[28] Ibid., p. 267.

approximations, inadequate as they are, will be worthwhile: the values are stable.[29]

Those values, in Pinto's case, are those of the Christian faith, and they are underpinned by his unquestioning belief in the Christian God and in divine Providence, which orders all things in accordance with God's mysterious plans, which are not in any way the same as man's. So, in the *Peregrinação*, there are numerous acts which the reader can recognize as good: acts of kindness, generosity and mercy. But it is not possible for a mere mortal to predict who will act in this way, or whether one good action will be followed by another. So it is that non-Christians will sometimes behave better than Christians, and sometimes the reverse. Underpinning it all is God or divine Providence — in Booth's view the supreme ironist, who understands where man cannot. Not all readers of the *Peregrinação* appreciate how thorough-going its ironies are, how the meaning of every event is countered by another event, and how the writer can find no complete explanation of anything outside the framework of the mysterious workings of Providence.

It is now time to explore the ironies of the Chinese boy episode more fully. As so often in the *Peregrinação*, the story begins with a shipwreck, on the aptly named Ilha dos Ladrões (Isle of Thieves). At this point in the narrative Pinto and the rest of the crew are under the command of António de Faria, a major figure in the book and one regarded by critics like Saraiva and Catz as one of the worst examples of European rapacity. Yet at first his behaviour is impeccable. He rallies the dispirited survivors, sets them to work burying the dead, and makes them an uplifting speech, pointing out to them the vanity of the things of this world (ch. 53; I, 167).

Yet Pinto's irony is unrelenting, and the reader is less convinced by Faria's speech when he learns that he made it while wearing a scarlet tunic which he had looted from one of the corpses. Yet, apparently, Providence favours the Portuguese. They are restored to health and strength by the discovery of meat and fish, the latter dropped obligingly by passing hawks. This is attributed by the narrator to divine intervention, and the hand of God seems even more present when they spot a Chinese boat whose crew, believing the island to be uninhabited, are resting on the shore. Faria urges his men to seize the boat with the holy name of Jesus on their lips and in their hearts, for in that 'depois de Deus, está a nossa salvação' (ch. 54; I, 171).[30] It seems an utterance of the grossest cynicism. The Chinese have done the Portuguese voyagers no harm; in fact, they are not even aware of their existence. And Pinto's use of irony to blame Faria seems borne out in the next chapter when the Chinese boy, left behind on the boat, rebukes his captors, both before and after his conversion, as explained above.

[29] Ibid., pp. 268–69.
[30] 'After God, is our salvation'.

And yet it is impossible to arrive at an overall judgement of Faria. The reader may well feel that the Chinese boy is right, but Faria's reaction to the criticism is not that of a criminal who has been accused by one of his victims. Instead, he invites the boy to convert. When the boy repeats his rebuke, now from the point of view of a committed Christian, Faria does not react angrily; in fact, he does not react at all, and the boy disappears from the narrative. In addition, as the modern writer Carlos Jorge has pointed out, Faria's piratical voyages had at least a gloss of legality, as he could be regarded as a privateer, preying legitimately on the enemies of the faith.[31] So John Christian Laursen is probably wrong to say that the reader is 'had', to use his terminology, and that Faria is no more than a criminal.[32] He is a criminal, but he is many other things besides, and the ironies surrounding him never cease.

We do not hear anything about the victim of another famous piratical act, the Chinese bride of chapter 47, who is abducted by António de Faria as she is on her way to meet her intended husband. The narrator allows her a moment of pity (I, 150), but never says what Faria's motive, be it sexual or financial, was in kidnapping her. He simply continues with further adventures, some of which contradict once again Faria's reputation for ferocity. This is particularly the case with chapter 48 — the one following the Chinese bride episode — in which the captain rewards some simple people because they belong to a group of monotheists, and are thus closer to being Christians than the majority of Asians. Yet the incident is no more than one of the hundreds of incomplete micro-narratives which form the superficial texture of the *Peregrinação*. It is given no special prominence, and Faria sails on for further adventures, and a highly ambiguous death.

From the incident of the Chinese boy and other related episodes one can point, in the first instance, to two ways in which Pinto creates situational ironies. The first is by the juxtaposition of the ups and downs of fortune, and of morally right and wrong actions, in a way which makes the relationship between them impossible to discern; consequently no overall moral judgements are possible. The individual acts which make up an episode may be good or bad, and recognizable as such, but they are always followed by some contrary act. The second is that the episodes never have a clear-cut ending, a fixed point from which to review, and judge, what has gone before. The last word is never said about anything. This is true of the structure of the *Peregrinação* as a whole, as well as of individual incidents.

The *Peregrinação* has seemed to some to be a religious book, a story of sin and redemption. The title is suggestive of a pilgrimage, from the medieval Latin 'peregrinus', and, from ch. 203 onwards, when Francis Xavier appears on

---

[31] Carlos Jorge Figueiredo Jorge, 'A dimensão da pirataria na *Peregrinação*: poder e contrapoder: uma ideologia da paródia', in *O discurso literário da Peregrinação: aproximações*, ed. by Maria Alzira Seixo and Christine Zurbach (Lisbon: Cosmos, 1999), pp. 63–93 (pp. 77–78, 90).
[32] Laursen, p. 29.

the scene, the narrative takes on a religious tone.[33] However, as many readers have noticed, the narrator experiences no change of heart, despite his evident admiration for the missionary. The historical Pinto may have joined the Jesuit order, and then left it, but no trace of those events appears in the *Peregrinação*. So the book is not the story of a personal journey to Christ. Nor are its final chapters the story of a historical process, with its beginning in the arrival of the first Jesuit missionaries in the East, and its end in the successful evangelization of Japan. The life of the narrator and the work of the missionaries are both unfinished business.

Everything revolves around the failed attempt to persuade the king of Bungo to convert. At the end of ch. 213 (already quoted), Xavier, victorious in theological disputation, leaves arm-in-arm with the king, but with the bonzes' curses ringing in his, and the reader's, ears. Immediately afterwards, and with the king still uncommitted, Xavier leaves Japan, to die an ignominious death on the coast of China, brought about in part by the squabbles of the Malacca Portuguese. Xavier is replaced by Pe. Belchior, a good man, though without Xavier's charisma. In ch. 225, the last chapter but one of the whole book, Belchior makes a final effort, and asks the king what would happen to his soul, should he die before converting. To this the king, prevaricating to the end, replies, with a smile: 'Deus o sabe' (II, 808).[34] They are words which might be said to sum up the whole meaning of the *Peregrinação*. There is irony, once again, in the way the reader is led to believe that the Jesuits will be successful, and yet invariably finds that belief to be unfounded.

After that the book moves rapidly to its close, in the next chapter. It has to end somewhere, after all, and Pinto's return to Portugal is a suitable point. However, the reader leaves the text with many questions unanswered. The ironic juxtaposition of the ups and downs of fortune continues, both in the public world of Jesuit missionizing and in the private world of Pinto's own life, in which his claim for a reward from the king is unmet, despite the support of the Governor of India, Francisco Barreto. Pinto ends, as he began, a devout though uncomprehending believer in the wisdom of God's Providence, and a sceptic with regard to the efficacy, and the permanence, of any human undertaking.

There is yet another way in which Pinto creates ironic doubt about the meaning of his text, and that is through variation in the point of view from which it is narrated. This is an aspect of the *Peregrinação* which has been much discussed, and there is no need to provide more than a summary here. A. J. Saraiva provides what is the fullest account of the variations in authorial point of view, from narrative in the first person singular, to narrative in the first person plural, when Pinto speaks as a member of a group, and finally to long sections narrated in the third person, where Pinto seems to disappear altogether.[35]

[33] See Laursen, p. 32, and the bibliography given there.
[34] 'God knows'.
[35] Saraiva, pp. 368–73.

Such variation makes it hard to ascribe authorial responsibility to statements in the text, and that responsibility is further deferred when Pinto uses oriental speakers to deliver moral judgements. Modern readers are inclined to believe that the judgements are valid, but it has already been suggested that Herrera Maldonado, for instance, did not see them in that way. Renaissance readers knew very well that not every speaker in a dialogue represented the author's personal viewpoint. To take, rather unusually, a theoretical statement made by a Portuguese writer, Damião de Góis, in his introduction to his version of the book of Ecclesiastes, he warns the reader that some of the statements made by Solomon, the supposed author of the book, are to be read as expressing his own views, while others are the opinions of the 'vulgo', the common herd. Since there is no obvious way of determining which statements are true and which are intended, ironically, to have the opposite of their surface meaning, the commentator has to intervene with his explanations. In general, the reader has to be on his guard.[36]

This is true even when faced by what seem to be obvious statements of moral truth, like those made by our old friend, the Chinese boy. It may be that António de Faria and his men, who include Pinto, are in gross dereliction of their Christian duty in their act of piracy. On the other hand, if they had not stolen the peaceful traders' vessel they would never have been able to continue their voyage — nor would Pinto have been able to continue his life. That his survival depends on a crime, one denounced by a mere child, is not the least of the ironies of his book.

What does Pinto intend by his endless ironies? For Wayne C. Booth, writing in the 1970s, the uncovering of ironic meanings was an aesthetic delight, and an end in itself: 'Each flash of ironic insight can lead us toward others, in a game never ending but always meaningful and entertaining'.[37] It may be that Booth is unconsciously reflecting the views of many readers of Pinto, certainly in the pre-modern period. Today, however, we live in a sterner age, in which mere literary pleasure is not enough.

What the modern reader encounters in the *Peregrinação* is doubt, not just the doubt, experienced by many over the centuries, as to the truthfulness or otherwise of the narrative, but doubts of many kinds, including metaphysical doubt. Why should the survival of a group of shipwrecked mariners depend on a crime? How can non-Christians have, on occasion, a greater degree of moral understanding than Christians? Why should an undoubtedly good and charismatic man — Francis Xavier — die ignominiously, his mission barely started? And so on.

It is clear that the answer to the doubts expressed in the book is not to assume, as Rebecca Catz did, that Mendes Pinto secretly opposed the standard

---

[36] Damião de Góis, *O Livro de Eclesiastes*, ed. by T. F. Earle (Lisbon: Fundação Calouste Gulbenkian, 2002), pp. 62–65.
[37] Booth, p. 269.

values of his age and nation. The *Peregrinação* is not a book which responds to a reductive reading, because it contains far too many loose ends. Rather, if the book expresses doubt, it is because its author, like many thoughtful people in Portugal in the second half of the sixteenth century, felt doubt, especially about the empire in the East.

FINAL NOTE. After this article was first submitted for publication I became aware of an interesting study by Catarina Fouto in the *Journal of Lusophone Studies*.[38] The methodology adopted by Dr Fouto is quite different from the rhetorical approach attempted here. However, her conclusions about the *Peregrinação*'s open-ended nature are very similar to mine, though she places less emphasis on Mendes Pinto's religious ideas, to me the most challenging aspect of his book. The two articles, taken together, will, I hope, make English-speakers aware that Mendes Pinto is an author for the twenty-first century.

---

[38] Catarina Fouto, 'Revisiting Baroque Poetics in Fernão Mendes Pinto's *Peregrinação*: The Poetics of Worldview', *Journal of Lusophone Studies*, 12 (2014), 65–88.

Geographical Knowledge and Mineral Riches in the Struggle for Sovereignty and Possession of Southern Brazil (1750–1755)

Denise Moura

State University of São Paulo (UNESP)

This article discusses the disputes between the Portuguese Crown and sertanistas [explorers of the *Sertão*, or hinterland] for the rights to explore and occupy the lands of the Tibagi sertões (which now form the state of Paraná, one of the three states in southern Brazil) and the relationship between this process and the accumulation of geographical knowledge of the area. The region contains a geopolitically strategic river network, formed by the eastern tributaries of the transnational River Paraná, which forms Brazil's natural border with Argentina and Paraguay and flows into the estuary of the River Plate, itself disputed at the time. These rivers, such as the River Iguaçu, which has its source in the town of Curitiba, provided access routes from the Tibagi sertões to the River Paraná and the towns close to the Atlantic coast, as can be observed in Map 1.

During the sixteenth century, the governor of Asunción, Hernando Aria de Saavedras, invited priests of the Society of Jesus to found missions in the valley of the Tibagi river, which has its source 200 km from Curitiba and flows into the River Paranapanema,[1] putting the Spanish at an advantage in terms of geographical knowledge of the area and physical progress into it. In turn, there were Luso-Brazilian sertanistas who had great practical knowledge of these lands, because they routinely travelled through them as though they were part of single regional unit extending from the city of São Paulo to the province of Guairá,[2] located on the banks of the River Plate.[3] They were attracted by its

---

[1] The missions San Francisco Xavier (1622), San José (1625), Encarnación (1625) and San Miguel (1626) were founded in this region, and then destroyed between 1628 and 1632 by the sertanistas from São Paulo (Jefferson de Lima Picanço and Maria José Mesquita, 'O sertão do Tibagi, os diamantes e o mapa de Angelo Pedroso Leme (1755)', *I Simpósio Brasileiro de cartografia histórica*, Paraty, 10 a 13 de maio de 2011, p. 5, online at <https://www.ufmg.br/rededemuseus/crch/simposio/PICANCO_JEFFERSON_E_MESQUITA_MARIA_JOSE.pdf> [accessed 2 January 2017]).
[2] Modern Paraguay.
[3] Sérgio Buarque de Holanda, 'Um mito geopolítico: a ilha Brasil', in *Tentativas de mitologias*, ed. by Sérgio Buarque de Holanda (São Paulo: Ed. Perspectiva, 1979), pp. 61–84 (p. 65).

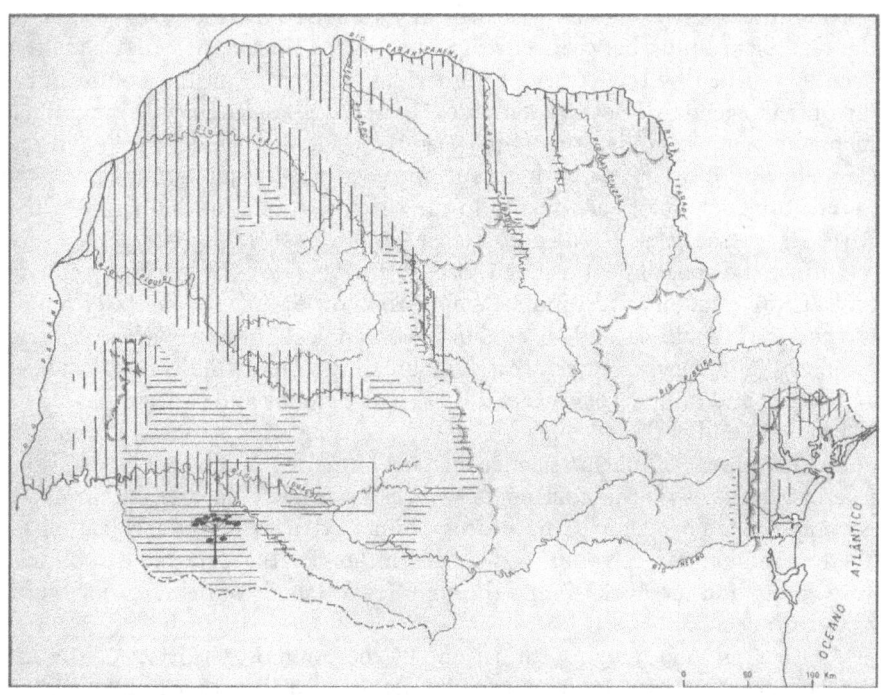

MAP 1. Rivers of Paraná state, reproduced by permission of the publishers from Jayme Antonio Cardoso and Cecília Maria Westphalen, *Atlas histórico do Paraná* (Curitiba: Livraria do Chain, Editora, 1986), p. 69. The Iguaçu River is marked with a box.

potential supply of indigenous labour[4] and its mineral wealth, since from 1600 to 1820 this region was the fourth largest gold producing region, after Minas Gerais, Goiás, and Mato Grosso, in that order.[5]

After the Iberian Union was officially dissolved in 1665, a revision of the territorial limits between Portugal and Spain in America that had first been established by the Treaty of Tordesillas (1494) was on the political and diplomatic agenda of both monarchies. In 1680, in an attempt to guarantee its presence in the lands situated between the Captaincy of São Paulo and the Captaincy of Rio Grande,[6] which encompassed the Tibagi sertões, Portugal founded the colony of Sacramento in the extreme south, on the banks of the River Plate estuary.[7]

During the government of Dom João V (r. 1707–1750), the Portuguese State took effective action to accumulate empirical knowledge of the Iberian frontier territories in America and to conduct geographical surveys with a view to establishing a new frontier treaty, mobilizing Jesuits, indigenous people, sertanistas and military engineers trained in geography and cartography.[8]

From the end of the seventeenth century, consolidation of ocean navigation and development of marine science enabled humanity to advance beyond the internal frontiers of the continents, which demanded that they accumulate geographical knowledge.[9] This process coincided with a standardization of Western diplomatic relations and a redefinition of the concept of political sovereignty and territorial limits through new methods of demarcation, such as topography.[10]

As early as 1609, Hugo Grotius, one of the foremost theorists of the *ius gentium* cited by eighteenth-century jurists, revised the criteria upon which ownership of the lands reached by the navigators was decided, denying the legality of the Iberian code hitherto applied to the navigation routes and the coastal territories that had been settled.[11] His writings associate sovereignty

---

[4] John Manuel Monteiro, *Negros da terra: índios e bandeirantes nas origens de São Paulo* (São Paulo: Companhia das Letras, 1995).
[5] Jefferson Picanço and Maria José Mesquita, 'A mineração aurífera na ocupação do planalto curitibano e litoral paranaense (séculos XVI–XVIII)', *Geosul*, 27.54 (2012), 117–37; Nestor Goulart Reis, *As minas de ouro e a formação das capitanias do sul* (São Paulo: Via das Artes, 2013), p. 53.
[6] Dauril Alden, *Royal Government in Colonial Brazil: With Special Reference to the Administration of the Marquis of Lavradio, Viceroy, 1769–1779* (Berkeley and Los Angeles: University of California Press, 1968), p. 59.
[7] Fabricio Prado, *Colônia do Sacramento: o extremo sul da América portuguesa* (Porto Alegre: Fumproarte, 2002).
[8] David M. Davidson, 'Rivers and Empire: The Madeira Route and the Incorporation of the Brazilian Far West, 1737–1808' (unpublished doctoral dissertation, Yale University, 1970); Beatriz Picolotto Siqueira Bueno, *Desenho e desígnio: o Brasil dos engenheiros militares (1500–1822)* (São Paulo: EDUSP/FAPESP, 2010).
[9] Margaret Deacon, *Scientists and the Sea: A Study of Marine Science* (London: Ashgate, 1997).
[10] Jaime Cortesão, *Alexandre de Gusmão & o Tratado de Madrid*, 2 vols (São Paulo: FUNAG/Imprensa Oficial, 2006), I, 92–93; Jeremy Black, *Maps and Politics* (Chicago, IL: University of Chicago Press, 1999), p. 127.
[11] Iris Kantor, 'Cartografia e diplomacia: usos geopolíticos da informação toponímica (1750–1850)',

with occupation, stating that lands

> [...] pertencem ao que as descobre e ocupa [...] o começo consiste na aplicação de um corpo a corpo, aplicação que, com relação às coisas imobiliárias, ocorre sobretudo por meio dos pés.[12]
>
> [[...] belong to those who discover and occupy them [...] the beginning consists of application of the body, an application which, in relation to matters of land, is achieved chiefly with the feet.]

Two principles widely employed by diplomats at the international negotiating tables to clothe their arguments with credibility were founded on this new conception of title by possession, based on the *uti possidetis* of Roman law: productive occupation and demonstration of geographical knowledge.[13]

After the Peace of Westphalia (1648), and particularly after the Treaties of Utrecht (1712–14), empirical geographical knowledge acquired by exploration *in loco* of lands and formalized in published texts and cartographic production became one of the bases of the agreements celebrated between European monarchies.[14] More recently, research has expanded this view and shown that these principles were also applied by those segments of society who lived in frontier regions under diplomatic dispute, who appealed to official authorities to defend what they believed to be their rights to possession of land and who were therefore, as much as the diplomats, also responsible for defining the territorial outlines of the Empires.[15] This article follows this line of interpretation in particular.

On the eve of the Treaty of Madrid (1750), formal knowledge of the lands in southern Brazil was insufficiently recorded in published texts and cartographic production. Maps that had been made of the region from the sixteenth century up to this point did not extend much further than the Paranaguá bay.[16] Once this first treaty had been signed and commissions nominated by both Crowns had been convened to confirm *in loco* the natural landmarks referred to in the document, the Portuguese Crown took the first official initiative to produce a plan for the exploration and occupation of the Tibagi sertões and to learn about

---

Anais do Museu Paulista, 17 (2009), 39–61 (p. 40), <http://www.scielo.br/scielo.php?script=sci_arttext&pid=S0101-47142009000200004> [accessed 8 January 2019].

[12] Hugo Grotius, *O direito da guerra e da paz (De jure belli ac Pacis, vol. I)* (Ijuí: Ed. Unijuí, 2004), p. 493.
[13] Júnia Furtado Ferreira, *Oráculos da geografia iluminista: Dom Luís da Cunha e Jean-Baptiste Bourguignon D'Anville na construção da cartografia do Brasil* (Belo Horizonte: Editora UFMG, 2012), p. 438.
[14] Furtado, *Oráculos*, p. 20.
[15] Tamar Herzog, *Frontiers of Possession: Spain and Portugal in Europe and the Americas* (Cambridge, MA: Harvard University Press, 2015), p. 236.
[16] Jefferson de Lima Picanço, 'A pesquisa mineral no século XVIII: o mapa da baía de Paranaguá de Pedro de Sousa Pereira (1653)', *II Simpósio luso-brasileiro de cartografia histórica*, Ouro Preto, 10 a 13 de novembro de 2009, <http://www.academia.edu/14848506/A_Pesquisa_Mineral_no_século_XVII_o_mapa_da_baía_de_Paranaguá_de_Pedro_de_Souza_Pereira_1653_The_Mineral_Exploration_in_seventeenth_century_The_map_of_Paranaguá_Bay_from_Pedro_de_Souza_Pereira_1653> [accessed 31 December 2016]; Jefferson de Lima Picanço and Maria José Mesquita 'O sertão do Tibagi, os diamantes e o mapa de Angelo Pedroso Leme (1755)', as note 1.

the courses of its river network, but this triggered reactions from the sertanistas and the local institutions, who began to lay official claim to the right to possess and use these sertões.

These disputes intensified once the Italian Francesco Tosi Colombina had been contracted to plan an expedition for the exploration and occupation of the Tibagi sertões, the manuscript agreement for which dates from 1752. In 1755, a sertanista called Angelo Pedroso Leme reacted by contracting a cartographer and, working together, they drew up a map to support a request for recognition of title to possession in the region. The project was transcribed and published, together with two other Notices, written by the Secretary of State for the Navy and Overseas Affairs, Diogo de Mendonça Corte Real, entitled 'Discovery of the Lands of Tibagi'.[17]

Rare transcriptions of these unique manuscripts[18] are held at the Guita and José Mindlin Library, belonging to the Institute of Brazilian Studies at the University of São Paulo, while the originals can be found in the manuscripts collection of the National Library.[19] However, in the papers of the Captaincy of São Paulo held in the Overseas Council digital archive, the Francesco Tosi Colombina manuscript is part of a dossier sent to Secretary Diogo de Mendonça[20] by the Ombudsman of the District of São Paulo, João de Sousa Filgueiras, that contains a total of ten documents including, among others, certificates from the sertanista, a petition containing accusations against Francesco Tosi, and letters and notes exchanged between Tosi and the viceroy Gomes Freire de Andrade. This dossier offers insights into the problems provoked by the Treaty of Madrid, such as the Portuguese Crown's realization of its ignorance of the Tibagi sertões and the extent to which its efforts to overcome this disadvantage provoked the sertanistas and local institutions.

Although it is often mentioned in historiography,[21] the Francesco Tosi Colombina manuscript is best known as a project that was planned, but never

---

[17] João Corrêa de Andrade and Carlos A. Neto, *Francisco Tosi Colombina: descobrimento das terras do Tibagi: manuscrito inédito do século XVIII* (Maringá: Universidade Estadual de Maringá, 1974), p. 1.

[18] A rare work can be defined according to a variety of different criteria. In this case, access to the edition is restricted because of the small number of copies and low circulation. Bruno Rizio Sant'Ana, 'Critérios para a definição de obras raras', *Revista on line Bibl. Prof. Joel Martins*, 3 (2001), 1–18 <http://www.ssoar.info/ssoar/bitstream/handle/document/10530/ssoar-etd-2001-3-santana-criterios_para_a_definicao_de.pdf> [accessed 6 April 2017].

[19] Andrade and Neto, *Francisco Tosi Colombina*, p. 1.

[20] 22 May 1755, São Paulo. Correspondence from the ombudsman of the district of São Paulo, João de Sousa Filgueiras, to the [Secretary of State for the Navy and Overseas Affairs] Diogo de Mendonça Corte Real, enclosing a certificate detailing what had been done about division of lands and licences for registration and requesting other royal decisions on the gold that had recently been discovered in the Tibagi sertão. Appended: petition (copy). AHU-São Paulo, cx. 4, doc. 28. AHU_ACL_CU_023_Cx 4, D. 282.

[21] Stephanie Laila Pires Souza, 'Francisco Tosi Colombina e o legado da engenharia militar: erudição e tradição na cartografia setecentista' <http://www.academia.edu/4850141/Francisco_Tosi_Colombina_e_o_Legado_da_Engenharia_Militar_erudição_e_tradição_na_cartografia_setecentista> [accessed 31 December 2016]; Riccardo Fontana, *Francesco Tosi Colombina: explorador, geógrafo, cartógrafo e engenheiro militar italiano no Brasil do século XVIII*, trans. by Edilson Alkmim Cunha (Brasília: n. pub., 2004), p. 19.

put into practice.²² The fact that this document has been under-utilized to answer the problems outlined above may be related to use of a copy without its original bureaucratic context, since it is common for documents to become separated from documents of other types to which they were originally related as part of the archiving process, with negative impacts on the way they are understood, their use in research, and their historical interpretation.

Thus, the manuscript contained in the dossier answers two questions that will be dealt with in this article. The first is related to the appointment of Francisco Tosi Colombina in the context of implementation of the Treaty of Madrid as a first royal initiative to attempt to overcome deficits in geographical knowledge of the Tibagi sertões. The second relates to the reactions against this initiative by sertanistas and municipal institutions, who attempted to defend their rights of possession and exploration in the region by drawing up public texts and cartographic materials.

An Italian-sertanista Geography

While the Italian Francesco Tosi Colombina has gained a certain notoriety over recent years, the principal references to his activities, in relation to the Portuguese development of geographical and in particular hydrographic knowledge of Brazil and their defence of political sovereignty, have been made outside of academia.²³

The multiplicity of the Genovese's abilities²⁴ is demonstrated by his many texts of a geopolitical nature, his cartographic work with an empirical foundation derived from his travels through the lands of Brazil, and by his works of military engineering, executed for the Portuguese Crown. His cartographic work is innovative²⁵ because his view that there was continuity between the hydrographic basins of Amazonas-Tapajós-Madeira-Mamoré and Paraná-Paraguay-River Plate did not fit the prevailing myth of Brazil as an island. His work was also advanced in comparison with the recognized mapmakers of the time, such as José Gonçalves da Fonseca, whose hydrographic maps only identified waterways as demarcation lines as far as the region of Mato Grosso.²⁶

Many claims and suppositions have been made about his biography that are unsupported by empirical evidence. There is no doubt, though, that the

---

²² Heloisa Liberalli Bellotto, *Autoridade e conflito no Brasil colonial: o governo do Morgado de Mateus em São Paulo (1765–1775)*, 2nd edn (São Paulo: Alameda, 2007), p. 136.
²³ Riccardo Fontana, *Francesco Tosi Colombina*.
²⁴ Fontana, *Francesco Tosi Colombina*, pp. 16–17.
²⁵ Jaime Cortesão, *História do Brasil nos velhos mapas*, tome II (Rio de Janeiro: Ministério das Relações Exteriores/Instituto Rio Branco, 1965), p. 267.
²⁶ André Ferrand de Almeida, 'A viagem de José Gonçalves da Fonseca e a cartografia do rio Madeira (1749–1752)', *Anais do Museu Paulista*, 17 (Jul–Dec 2009), 215–35, <http://www.scielo.br/scielo.php?script=sci_arttext&pid=S0101-47142009000200011> [accessed 31 December 2016].

Portuguese court did indeed seek out specialists in geography, cartography, mathematics, and astronomy in Italian cities, including the mathematician Father Domenico Capacci and the geographer Michelangelo Blasco. Cortesão claims that Tosi was a geographer and professor of geography and Fontana has concluded that his services were recommended by the mathematician and engineer from Modena, Domenico Vandelli, and by Michelangelo Blasco,[27] to collaborate with the Lisbon Court on their projects for expansion and recognition of the western border of Brazil.

On a geographical map that he made in 1756 and dedicated to Secretary of State Tomé Joaquim da Costa Corte Real, Francesco Tosi Colombina states that he was honoured that the Secretary had listened to his Geography lessons and accepted him as his teacher.[28] However, there is insufficient empirical evidence to permit conclusions about his academic studies and work, in contrast with his experience in the field, i.e., his demonstration of detailed topographic knowledge gained by observation *in loco*, such as rivers and their directions of flow, which was a premise of the concept of 'practical fieldwork' systematized by the prevailing Portuguese school of military engineering,[29] which involved detailed surveys to acquire topographical information before starting work in the bureau. This method demanded the use of the appropriate instruments,[30] which Francesco Tosi did not possess, conducting his surveys by observation and by gleaning information from the local sertanistas.

In the text of his project, Francesco Tosi Colombina requested a commission as sergeant-major of Engineers, the degree of Royal Geographer, and the instruments necessary to carry out the task.[31] The requests were granted by the King on 10 September 1753, which indicates that when he entered Brazil he had not yet been officially contracted and did not hold these titles.

Francesco Tosi justified his request by his two years of service as Tenant at Arms to the Queen of Prussia, when he had taken part in two campaigns in Italy fighting against the French.[32] His references, therefore, were not for academic and scientific services in Portugal, but as a professional with practical experience on the battlefield, where success was also conditional on reasonable and calculated knowledge of the terrain, as suggested by ancient texts on the art of war translated and published in Europe in the eighteenth century.[33]

During this period in Europe, many border conflicts took place and the trenches became a type of classroom where soldiers and officers learnt geography, artillery and engineering, and developed their skills in topograph-

---

[27] Cortesão, *História do Brasil nos velhos mapas*, p. 268; Fontana, *Francesco Tosi Colombina*, p. 18.
[28] Cortesão, *História do Brasil nos velhos mapas*, p. 317.
[29] Cortesão, *História do Brasil nos velhos mapas*, p. 289.
[30] Bueno, *Desenho e desígnio*, pp. 103–23.
[31] Andrade and Neto, *Francisco Tosi Colombina*, p. 37.
[32] Andrade and Neto, *Francisco Tosi Colombina*, p. 37.
[33] There are many such examples, but the most notable is 'The Art of War', by Sun Tzu, translated from the Chinese by the priest Jean Amiot, in 1772.

ical observation and measurement of lands and rivers, without the precision and rigour of the conventions of mathematical geography, but with enough detail for preliminary reconnaissance of routes and lands.

Francesco Tosi's justifications for his requests also evinced empirical experience in lands in America, since, as he himself stated, with the titles granted and the command of the expeditions to people the lands of Tibagi, he would feel rewarded for everything that he had 'feito em dez anos na América para reconhecimento dela' [done in ten years in America for her reconnaissance].[34] Francesco Tosi promised that if he was granted command of the mission, as he in fact was, he would make a map for the King.[35] Thus, Francesco Tosi's knowledge of geography and cartography was initially acquired on the battlefields of Europe and later built upon in America, where the vast unknown sertões were an ideal place to acquire new skills.

The scenario of disputes between the Monarchies of Europe to define their borders created the political will to recognize and exhort to action these explorers, like Francesco Tosi, who were responsible for formalizing in public texts and cartographic materials the shapes of the internal borders of the overseas possessions and who contributed to the role played by Iberians in European sciences, in the fields of physical geography and continental cartography.[36]

Francesco Tosi's plan also represents the start of the Crown's activities to promote occupation and possession, affirming its sovereignty in the sertões of southern Brazil, since, as Tosi himself stated, the King had decided that 'se povoem, e estabeleçam as terras do Tabagy' [the lands of Tabagi be peopled and established], nominating him for an expedition and, following royal orders, he expounds in manuscript the 'meyos, que são mais precisos e o modo como se deve executar esta empresa' [means that are most precise and the methods by which this enterprise should be executed].[37]

For Francesco Tosi, then, the question was not one of 'discovery', or of being a 'discoverer' of these lands that had been known and traversed for a long time, but of making Portugal their 'master', i.e. of taking possession of those lands,[38] which presupposes that they are already known. For him, the idea of 'discoveries' was associated rather with mineral riches. Colombina thus formalized a status of 'discoverers' of minerals that would guarantee the Crown the right of priority in their exploitation. Nevertheless, the legitimate occupation that justified exploitation was increasingly associated with a demonstration of geographical knowledge.

[34] Andrade and Neto, *Francisco Tosi Colombina*, p. 31.
[35] Andrade and Neto, *Francisco Tosi Colombina*, p. 37.
[36] Essential reading for those interested in the Iberian contribution to development of modern science is Jorge Cañizares-Esguerra, *Nature, Empire, and Nation: Explorations of the History of Science in the Iberian World* (Stanford, CA: Stanford University Press, 2006).
[37] Andrade and Neto, *Francisco Tosi Colombina*, p. 31.
[38] Andrade and Neto, *Francisco Tosi Colombina*, p. 33.

Francesco Tosi Colombina was invited to plan this project by the Governor and Captain-General of the Captaincy of Rio de Janeiro, Gomes Freire de Andrade, who had a thorough knowledge of the geographic potential of the lands of southern Brazil through his thirty years in government (1733–63). Additionally, at the time that he extended this invitation to Tosi, Gomes Freire chaired the sub-commission for the South, charged, for the Portuguese side, with confirming *in loco* the landmarks demarcating the territorial limits between Portugal and Spain in America that had been defined by the Treaty of Madrid. The Iberian sub-commissions began work on 8 October 1752, but Francesco Tosi was not a member of the team of military engineers, astronomers, cartographers, mathematicians and geographers.

Portugal was not sufficiently technically developed to conduct this work, despite the investments in teaching geographic science in Military Academies throughout the Joanine period. As a result, many of the professionals who made up these commissions were contracted at Italian universities, such as Bologna, Padua, Rome, Verona, Venice, Florence and Milan, and also in Paris, Basel and Vienna.

Since the Portuguese commission had to work with the Spanish commission, travelling in the field to confirm the geographic landmarks and install markers on the borders, a freelance contract such as the engagement of Francesco Tosi could have been a strategy for the Portuguese Crown to bring forward a plan for the occupation and exploration of a region rich in mineral resources and with a hydrographic network offering access routes to rivers designated as natural borders whose sources, falls and course were as yet unknown. For example, a few leagues from the falls on the Iguaçu river was the source of the Santo Antonio river, that flowed into the Pepiriguaçu, which in turn was a territorial landmark. Neither Crown had sufficient geographical knowledge of these watercourses, as shown by the disagreements and arguments between the two commissions that proved to be one of the causes of the dissolution of the Treaty of Madrid in 1763.[39]

The Treaty of Madrid may therefore have been a strategy for the Portuguese Crown to buy time and create mechanisms to solve their knowledge deficits, as shown by the freelance engagement of Francesco Tosi, since in him the Portuguese Crown acquired a servant with geographical knowledge acting on the fringes of the border commissions and, therefore, with greater freedom to observe the lands it was claiming.

The geopolitical need for knowledge of the topography of the Tibagi sertões, and especially of their hydrographic network, therefore derived from two problems: how to define the territorial limits of Portugal and Spain in America and how to guarantee the right to exploit the region's mineral resources, the

---

[39] Alden, *Royal Government*, pp. 86–96; Fábio Kuhn, *Gente da fronteira: família e poder no continente do Rio Grande (Campos de Viamão, 1720–1800)* (São Leopoldo: Oikos, 2014), pp. 79–88.

initial phase of which took place in the river beds themselves, particularly the extraction of gold.[40]

In tune with the interests of the Crown, but also aware of the sertanistas' knowledge, and referring to the ancient myth that the natural riches of a place accumulate where the sun sets,[41] Francesco Tosi began his project declaring that he intended to examine the lands of Tibagi, which lay to the west of São Paulo, to discover whether 'há nellas aquella grandesa de ouro que promettem as experiências dos velhos sertanistas' [there is in them the quantities of gold promised by the experience of the ancient sertanistas].[42]

As such, territorial knowledge accumulated by the sertanistas and by indigenous people provided the basis for the geography and the logistics of this Italian's exploration and occupation of the Tibagi sertões, responsible for formulating an Italian-sertanista geography, in other words, one that combined the geographical knowledge of a soldier from the trenches of Europe with that of the populations living in the lands of Brazil. Colombina's experience in the Prussian army, supposedly during the 1730s, during the reigns of Frederick William I and Sophia Dorothea of Hanover, and on the battlefields of Italy, prompted him to invoke the negative memories he had of a French general who attributed an Army's victories exclusively to money, whereas for him, Francesco Tosi, what was relevant were guns, gunpowder and lead, i.e. the tools of war, combined with the disposition and experience of the Paulistas, i.e. knowledge of the practices of the sertão.

This sensitivity to and confidence in empirical experience of the land could have their origins in the characteristics of the Italian's training, i.e. have been forged in his twin observations and passages through the trenches of Europe and the sertões of Brazil, where he named his sources of information, suggesting that he had been in personal contact with sertanistas. As he stated explicitly, the success of this venture lay in the 'vontade dos Paulistas [...] que hão de fazer o que costumão em semelhantes occasioens' [will of the Paulistas [...] who must do what they have done on similar occasions].[43] It therefore depended on the support received, i.e., in terms of financial resources to carry out the project, and the Crown should grant what it saw fit, since will and knowledge were enough for people such as Pascoal Moreira Cabral, Miguel Sutil de Oliveira, and João Godoy da Silveira Preto, who had discovered the Mines of Cuibá, of Paranapanema, or of Pillar.[44]

---

[40] Sérgio Buarque de Holanda, 'Metais e pedras preciosas', in *História geral da civilização brasileira: a época colonial*, ed. by Sérgio Buarque de Holanda, 4th edn (São Paulo: DIFEL/Difusão Editorial, 1977), pp. 259–310.
[41] Sérgio Buarque de Holanda, *Visão do paraíso: os motivos edênicos no descobrimento e colonização do Brasil*, 5th edn (São Paulo: Editora Brasiliense, 1992), p. 101.
[42] Andrade and Neto, *Francisco Tosi Colombina*, p. 31.
[43] Ibid.
[44] Andrade and Neto, *Francisco Tosi Colombina*, p. 32.

The rare topographic sensibility of the indigenous people[45] surpassed in strategic value any sum of money, because Tosi considered that the project would be successful if it relied on the 'Guayaná People' who, fleeing from the aforementioned Paulistas, had taken refuge in the sertões and promised 'discoveries of gold', as he claimed to have witnessed when they were promised that they would not be enslaved.

The Genovese's geography was based on twin sources of information, i.e., on observation of the terrain and on contact with indigenous people and sertanistas, but he was also a strategist, since he was in favour of taking advantage of local human resources when exploring and he reused the lessons learned in other Captaincies and on the Prussian battlefields, proposing the formation of military companies:

> Companhia de Soldados ventureiros, ou Pedestres de Bastardos, Mulatos, e outros accostumados à Sertanejar, como huma que de presente se acha em Goyas; e Minas Gerais, para observar, se há quem estraya diamantes naquelles sertões, e que tanto os ditos Soldados, quanto os seus Officiais Brancos.[46]

> [Company of adventurer Soldiers, or Infantry of Bastards, Mulattoes, and others accustomed to the Sertões, like one that can be found in Goyas; and Minas Gerais, to observe, if there is anyone extracting diamonds in those sertões, and this applies to both these Soldiers, and their White Officers.]

The rivers of the Tibagi sertão had been identified as routes for accessing a region of minerals, rich in gold, and as waterways that communicated directly with the River Paraná, since in an undated note appended to the dossier Gomes Freire stated that Tosi was waiting to hear 'das canoas que [mandara] descer ao salto do Paraná e levar principal recomendação para examinar se havia ou não ouro nas paragens por onde passem como primeiramente haviam de tocar as bocas do Tabagi' [about the canoes that [he had ordered to] go down to the Paraná falls with the principal mission of examining whether there was gold in the places through which they pass, as they first had to pass the mouths of the Tabagi].

In addition to the gold, one of the project's primary objectives was to survey the courses of the rivers since, as Tosi had stated, the expedition would start from the town of Sorocaba, march sixty leagues along the route to Curitiba:

> com rumo de Sudoeste até onde as cabeceiras do rio Tabagy atravessão tal caminho, se deve acompanhar dito Rio algumas quarenta Légoas, com rumo ao Nord até dar na altura de Sorocaba, que verá a ver no meyo do Supe da corda da dita Serra, que corre do Rio Grande de Curitiba até o Rio Paraná.[47]

---

[45] Cortesão, *Alexandre de Gusmão*, pp. 304, 307.
[46] Andrade and Neto, *Francisco Tosi Colombina*, p. 34.
[47] Andrade and Neto, *Francisco Tosi Colombina*, p. 35.

[towards the Southwest to where the headwaters of the Tabagy river cross the route, from where the river should be followed for some forty Leagues, in a Northerly direction up to the level of Sorocaba, which will be seen in the middle of the foothills of the range that runs from the Rio Grande of Curitiba to the river Paraná.]

The Crown's intention in contracting the services of a professional who could enable the Portuguese to overcome their deficit in regional hydrographic knowledge is evident in the following speculation by Tosi: 'Este novo caminho **deve** ter muitos rios que o atravessam, mais que no que vay para Curitiba, e mayores, porque todas as vertentes, que nascem da Serra da Costa do mar, correm para o Norte para buscar o rio Paraná' [This new route **must** be crossed by many rivers that do not go to Curitiba, and are larger, because all of the branches that have their source in the coastal range run to the North to meet the River Paraná].[48] Here, Francesco Tosi is also expressing a conceptualization of the interconnected functions of primary rivers and tributaries which, with the advent of modern hydrographic science, would come to be known as hydrographic basins and would change the way rivers were seen in management of water resources.[49]

Tosi saw the longest river in the Tibagi region, the Iguaçu, as a possible obstacle to penetration by the Spanish, which is one of the issues that had concerned the Portuguese Crown since the seventeenth century, when it encouraged sertanistas from São Paulo to make violent incursions against the missions. However, as he wrote, the northern part of this river had been explored and it was known that there was a mountain range to the north and those settling the region should people the entire eastern extent of the range 'e sirvão de impedimento aos que moram na parte ocidental, de poder atravessar a mesma ou de comunicação com eles' [serving as an impediment to those living on the western side, preventing them from crossing and from communicating].[50]

Although Francesco Tosi is better known for his connections to the governor of the recently created Captaincy of Goiás in 1748, D. Marcos de Noronha, and for making the first cartographic representation of the region, in 1751,[51] he was also responsible for establishing the foundations of Portuguese empirical hydrography of the Tibagi sertões, formalized in public texts.

On the basis of his observations of the courses of the region's rivers, Francesco Tosi concluded that this hydrographic network provided access from the Serra do Mar coastal mountain range, i.e. from the coast, to the most important river of the River Plate basin, the River Paraná. He thus provided the Portuguese with hydrographic information that allowed them to anticipate any

[48] Andrade and Neto, *Francisco Tosi Colombina*, p. 36. My emphasis.
[49] Augusto Romera e Silva, *Água: quem vive sem?*, 2nd edn (São Paulo: FCTH/CT-Hidro, 2003).
[50] Andrade and Neto, *Francisco Tosi Colombina*, p. 33.
[51] Deusa Maria Rodrigues Boaventura, 'Urbanização de Goiás na primeira metade do século XVIII: a cartografia e a construção do território', *IX Seminário de história da cidade e do urbanismo* (unpublished conference paper, São Paulo, 4 to 6 September 2006).

Spanish attempt to penetrate southern Brazil via the south coast. Hydrography and sovereignty were therefore two key elements of this manuscript written by Francesco Tosi, which concerned sertanistas and local institutions who were already exploring and claiming rights of possession in the region.

A Technical-sertanista Cartography

In 1755, armed with a certificate and a map made by the cartographer Manuel Angelo Figueira de Aguiar (see Map 2), Angelo Pedroso Leme, a sertanista from São Paulo, attended an audience with the ombudsman of the district of São Paulo, João de Sousa Filgueiras, to officially request recognition of his right to exploit the Tibagi sertões, of which he claimed to be one of the first discoverers. The original of this map is in the Archive of Overseas History, Lisbon, and there are two copies in Brazil, one in the Archive of Army History and the other in the Itamaraty map library, which was made in 1910.[52]

The certificate contains attempts to justify the request that demonstrate that the concepts of possession of land based on occupation and indication of knowledge of its topography echoed with several different social strata, including those that were not part of the elite of diplomats and royal appointees who also took part in processes of territorial formation in the eighteenth century and in the production of formal geographic knowledge of lands subject to diplomatic disputes.

Many public texts, such as letters, reports, travel narratives, or court proceedings justify possession of land on the basis of occupation with crop cultivation or animal husbandry,[53] which acquire greater authority and credibility when combined with maps, and both ambassadors and private individuals involved in issues of territorial possession used these written and visual instruments.

The certificate presented by Angelo Pedroso Leme states that he is a native of the city of São Paulo and that he had left nine years previously, to go to the 'River Tibagi sertão' where he began to 'fazer descobrimentos de ouro com incansável trabalho que se sabe tem os descobridores em sertões novos e incógnitos' [make discoveries of gold with the tireless labour that is well known of the discoverers of new and unknown sertões], stating that he had discovered 'vários ribeirões com suas pintas de ouro' [many streams speckled with gold] which he wished to report to the ombudsman, who was also the auditor general and superintendent for gold.

Describing his gold extraction activities in the Tibagi sertões, the sertanista demonstrated that he had topographical and hydrographic information about the region. He said, for example, that the gold he had extracted over the years

---

[52] Isa Adonias (ed.), *Mapa: imagens da formação territorial brasileira* (Rio de Janeiro: Fundação Odebrecht, 1993), p. 288.
[53] Herzog, *Frontiers*, pp. 33–34 and 41–42.

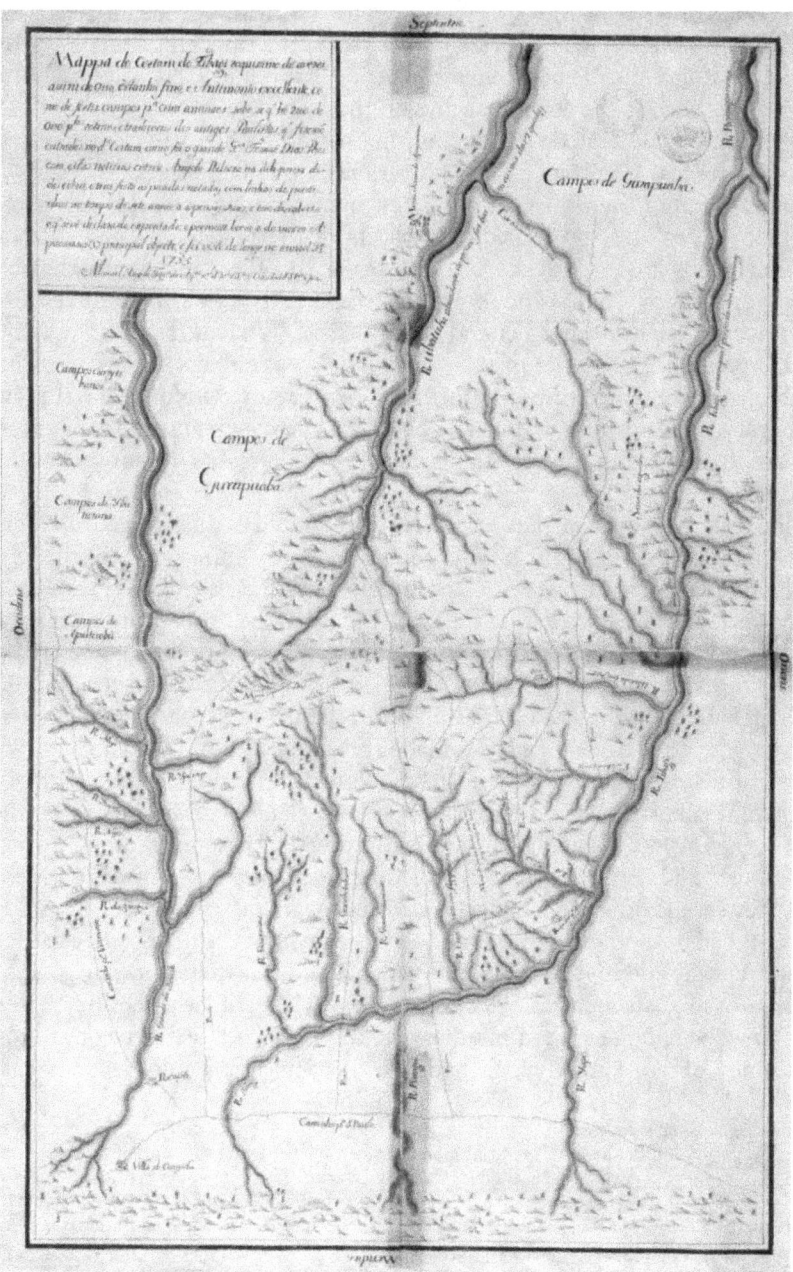

MAP 2. Map of the Sertão do Tibagi by Manuel Angelo Figueira de Aguiar (1755), reproduced by permission of its owners, the Archivo Histórico Ultramarino, Lisbon.

had been found in the area 'modea entre o rio Tibagi e o rio Grande do Registro de Viamão' [between the River Tibagi and the Rio Grande of Registro de Viamão] and that he had undertaken to discover the Apucarana hill but had not examined it for 'falta de mantimentos' [lack of provisions]. He at least indicated its location both in the certificate and on the map.

Angelo Pedroso stated that during this period he had had 'experiência em vários córregos, ribeirões e rios' [experiences in many creeks, streams and rivers] and from them he had extracted many samples of gold, citing many of their names and the respective weights of the nuggets he had extracted, demonstrating his experience of the terrain, in other words, his knowledge of its topography, the locations, nature and quality of its mineral resources, such as the weight of nuggets and the routes of watercourses. This was not a land survey in the manner of the professional geographers trained at military academies,[54] and carried out with instruments and techniques for surveying topographical information, but one based on the concrete activity of entering the creeks, removing minerals, and entering the terrain to examine hills and mountains.

The sertanista ends by requesting he be appointed as interim guardian of the 'ditas minas novas de Tabagi' [aforementioned new mines of Tabagi], so that 'nellas não se façam distrações [...] e para que se vá fixar as repartições das datas das ditas terras minerais' [from them nothing shall be misappropriated [...] and so that apportionment of the deposits in these areas of minerals can be fixed],[55] providing evidence of a type of procedure already identified by historiographers, i.e., deriving the right to administrate from the first discovery.[56]

One year after Angelo Pedroso made this request of the ombudsman of the district of São Paulo, the ombudsman in turn wrote to the Secretary of the Kingdom, Sebastião José de Carvalho e Melo (later the Marquis of Pombal), describing the local disputes over these discoveries. He stated that the Governor of Santos[57] had urged on the town of Curitiba, district of Paranaguá, writing that they should 'tomar posse das terras do Tabagi' [take possession of the lands of Tabagi]. The ombudsman claimed that the town of Curitiba had been incited to appropriate the discovery 'contra a vontade do descobridor, obrigando-o a fazer novo texto de manifesto' [contrary to the wishes of the discoverer, obliging him to write another text in manifestation]. The Tibagi sertão belonged to the Captaincy of São Paulo, which had two districts, São Paulo, with its capital

---

[54] Bueno, *Desenho e desígnio*.
[55] 22 May 1755, São Paulo. Letter from the ombudsman of the district of São Paulo, João de Sousa Filgueiras, to [Secretary of state for the Navy and Overseas Affairs] Diogo de Mendonça Corte Real, sending the certificate detailing what had been done in terms of division of lands, licences for mining, and requesting other royal decisions with respect to the recently discovered gold in the Tibagi sertão. Appended: petition (copy). AHU-São Paulo, cx. 4, doc. 28. AHU_ACL_CU_023_Cx 4, D. 282.
[56] Adriana Romeiro, *Paulistas e emboabas no coração das minas: idéias, práticas e imaginário político no século XVIII* (Belo Horizonte: Editora UFMG, 2008).
[57] He refers to the military governor of the port of Santos, on the south coast of the Captaincy of São Paulo.

in the city of the same name and situated in the elevations above the town of Santos, and the district of Paranaguá, located on the southern coast, to which the town in the hills above, Curitiba, was affiliated.

The dispute over this region therefore also involved institutions of local power, which could explain why the sertanista took the precaution of arming himself with written documents and maps to defend his interests in the rights of possession. In this case, Manuel Figueira's map, which specialists in the history of cartography generally analyse in isolation,[58] should be considered in association with the certificate, since together, if interpreted in the light of the theoretical principles of the history of cartography[59] express the sertanista's concept of space and of rights over it, and of the cartographer's art, since 'the cognitive nature of the act of mapmaking' qualifies it as a 'a memory bank of part perceptions or mental images',[60] i.e., as something beyond a mere Euclidean record of the arduous reality of the topography.

This map translates into the language of cartography the information in the sertanista's certificate, which may explain the absence of measures of distance between the different elements on the map, such as between Registro and the town of Curitiba, the sertanista's farm and the River Tibagi. For example, there are no indications of the breadth or length of creeks, rivers or streams, or measures of degrees of longitude, so this is not a map with scientific pretensions, or one intended to guide travels through the region; it is rather to provide evidence of knowledge of the topographical characteristics of the place. In other words, in conjunction with the certificate, the map was confirmation that the sertanista knew of the existence of mountains, the silhouettes of creeks and streams, and the major rivers that made up the region.

However, this map, as a hybrid artefact,[61] made by two different people, also bears the marks of a professional cartographer and, in contrast with what some authors have concluded,[62] this is not a simple map since it reveals familiarity with symbols of the cartographic conventions of the epoch; as the seventeenth and eighteenth centuries progressed, there was a process of 'consolidação de convenções e códigos de representação cartográfica e topográfica' [consolidation of conventions and codes of cartographic and topographic representation] which tended to replace the free illustrations previously employed.[63]

---

[58] Picanço and Mesquita, 'O sertão do Tibagi, os diamantes e o mapa de Angelo Pedroso Leme (1755)'.
[59] M. J. Blakemore and J. B. Harley, *Concepts in the History of Cartography: A Review and Perspective* (= *Cartographica*, 17.4 (winter 1980)), monograph 26 (Toronto: University of Toronto Press, 1980); J. B. Harley, 'Silences and Secrecy: The Hidden Agenda of Cartography in Early Modern Europe', *Imago Mundi*, 40 (1988), 56–76.
[60] Blakemore and Harley, *Concepts*, p. 97.
[61] This map provides evidence, on a small scale, of the character of multiple authorship of eighteenth-century mapmaking, as demonstrated by some historians in relation to the maps used in diplomatic negotiations. Neil Safier, *Measuring the New World: Enlightenment Science and South America* (Chicago, IL: University of Chicago Press, 2008), chap. 5.
[62] Picanço and Mesquita, 'O sertão do Tibagi, os diamantes e o mapa de Angelo Pedroso Leme (1755)', p. 6.
[63] Bueno, *Desenho e desígnio*, p. 307.

The cartographer used representations of trees, and distinguished mounds and hills with their own designs. The sertanista's conception of the sertão, translated by the quill of the cartographer, was of a space administered by the royal public authority, since the registry office labelled with the name of the town of Curitiba, where taxes were levied on flocks of animals, is represented by a drawing of a building. Nevertheless, the Portuguese State was not seen as the holder of the legitimate right to mastery over those lands, since the sertanista associated this right with demonstration of knowledge of their geography and with their exploitation, such as extraction of gold from creeks and streams, as demonstrated by the map.

The town of Curitiba is represented by a drawing of a church, which indicated both that the immediate perception of the inhabitants of Portugal's overseas domains in relation to local powers was most strongly associated with the parish, and also indicates the sertanista's intention in emphasizing his rights to possession to the detriment of the municipal authority. In contrast to a parish, a municipality could claim rights over lands beyond its municipal limits, which officially corresponded to six leagues from the town hall.[64]

Angelo Pedroso's farm was indicated by a more detailed drawing of a building, with a door and windows and the roof coloured in, than was used for another farm, situated further up on the banks of the River Ubatuba, and therefore a long way from the major river, the Tibagi, which was represented with a drawing of a village dwelling.[65]

There are also no human references in this technical-sertanista map, such as the indigenous groups who certainly lived in the region, because its function was not to indicate precautions needed when travelling through the area, nor to indicate the existence of possible vassals and Christians for the Catholic Portuguese Monarchy, but to emphasize Angelo Pedroso's fixed and regular productive activity in the region as part of a judicial petition.

From the point of view of its compositional and iconographic characteristics,[66] observe the silhouettes of the major rivers, such as the Tibagi and the Rio Grande do Registro,[67] and of their tributaries, which form the outlines of the aquatic line that crossed the as yet undiscovered sertões of Guarapuava.

To the extent that maps are a 'selective representation of reality' and the cartographer is more a 'creator', than a 'reflector', maps are also instruments of power and of communication of certain interests, such as those of ownership and

---

[64] Raquel Glezer, *Chão de terra e outros ensaios sobre São Paulo* (São Paulo: Ed. Alameda, 2007), pp. 91–109.
[65] For this analysis I used copies of codes published by Beatriz Bueno from a work by François Dainville, *Le Langage des Géographes*, who, according to Beatriz, conducted an exhaustive survey of the codes and symbols of Western cartographic representation in the seventeenth and eighteenth centuries. Bueno, *Desenho e desígnio* p. 309.
[66] Erwin Panofsky, 'Iconografia e iconologia: uma introdução ao estudo da arte da renascença', in *Significado nas artes visuais* (São Paulo: Ed. Perspectiva, 1979), pp. 47–87.
[67] Another name for the River Iguaçu.

territorial rights.[68] Manuel Figueira's map, therefore, expressed the sertanista's assertion of his rights deriving from primacy of occupation and possession of lands in southern Brazil that the Portuguese Crown was practically ignorant of, but which it was beginning to organize itself to explore.

The emphasis the mapmaker gives to the river network of the Tibagi sertões is related to the sertanista's assertion in the certificate of his primacy in discovery and exploitation of the gold deposits, including the claim that he knew the toponymy of its rivers, streams and creeks. On the map, several streams are labelled with phrases indicative of their potential for the extraction of gold. By the River Capivari, for example, one of the tributaries of the Tibagi, there appears the phrase 'gold panning', by the River Ubatuba it is noted that there is 'panning', and by another stream is recorded simply 'gold seen', showing the different levels of gold extraction undertaken by the sertanista in the region, i.e., in some places panning for gold was already ongoing, in others there was only knowledge that gold was present.

The courses of the region's rivers on the map do not represent the topographic reality, but the intentions of the cartographer and the sertanista. Therefore, the source of the Tibagi river, which was originally in the mid-south of the current state of Paraná, appears in the coastal mountain range on this map, outside of the area of influence of the town of Curitiba and along the 'route to São Paulo', the sertanista's hometown.

Three dotted lines, representing routes travelled, run from Angelo Pedroso's farm on the east bank of the River Tibagi and cross all of the creeks, streams and rivers where there are records of gold deposits. In contrast, the only other farm shown on the map does not have any dotted lines, showing the intention of emphasizing the image of this sertanista as an explorer. As stated in the certificate, he, Angelo Pedroso, dedicated himself to discovering gold in the region with 'tireless labour', just as the discoverers of 'new and unknown sertões' had done. On the map, his farm has been drawn at the closest point to the gold seams and the stream that ran beside his stream had gold on its 'banks' and Pedra Branca hill, situated in an area within reach of his farm, had gold on all of its 'slopes'.

Since the municipal authorities of the towns of Curitiba and of São Paulo were also involved in the dispute for the right to administrate the region, the cartographer's intention was to demonstrate with the dotted line that there was no trail (*picada*) from the town of Curitiba in the direction of the gold-bearing streams and the Tibagi sertões. In other words, that the people from that region had no involvement in the discoveries. In contrast, Angelo Pedroso's farm was not only shown with dotted lines that traversed the whole of the gold-bearing hydrographic basin of Tibagi, but was also on the 'route to São Paulo'.

---

[68] Jeremy Black, *Maps and Politics*, pp. 11 and 18.

In Luso-Brazilian cartography and geography, the drawing of Angelo Pedroso Leme's farm or communication of his knowledge of the toponymy and topography were not alone sufficient to arm his arguments with credibility and so the fundamentals of tradition were also employed, such as the ancient sertanistas who had travelled the region and were even mentioned on the map's cartouche:

> Mappa do Certam do Tibagi riquissimo de averes assim de oiro, estanho fino e Antimonio Excelente, como de fertiz campos para criar animaes: **sabe-se que hé rico de oiro, pelos roteiros, e tradiçoens dos antigos paulistas que fizerão entradas no dito Certam: como foi o grande Governador Fernão Dias Paes com estas noticias entrou Angelo Pedrozo na diligencia de descobrir e tem feito as picadas notadas com linhas de pontinhos no tempo de sete annos a espensas suas**; e tem descoberto o que se vê declarado e apontado e promette breve o do morro Alpucarana (1) principal objecto e foi visto de longe no anno de 1754/55. [My emphasis.]

> [Map of the Tibagi Sertão, with great riches in gold, in fine tin and Excellent Antimony, and fertile fields for raising animals: **it is known that it is rich in gold, from the routes and traditions of the ancient Paulistas who entered the said Sertão: such as the great Governor Fernão Dias Paes and with this news Angelo Pedrozo entered, diligent to discover, and created the trails marked in dotted lines over a period of seven years at his own expense**; and has discovered what is hereby declared and described and promises soon the same for Alpucarana hill (1) principal objective, which was seen from a distance in the year 1754/55.]

This conferred the cartography of Manuel Angelo Filgueira de Aguiar with trustworthiness because it followed reports by ancient paulistas from the town of São Paulo, and was not, therefore, the product of a simple adventure, while, by evoking the contribution made by the paulistas to the geography of the region, the cartographer contributes to consolidating a tradition of groups from the town of São Paulo, rather than from Curitiba. However, the cartography of Manuel Angelo and the geography of Francesco Tosi also demonstrate that diplomacy and the advancement of geographical knowledge about the internal borders of the continents in the eighteenth century did not only gather diplomats and royal authorities around these professionals, but also involved native populations and sertanistas.

This article forms part of a research project conducted within the Research Residency Program at the Biblioteca Brasiliana Guita e José Mindlin, USP, from September 2015 to September 2016, entitled 'Nas águas do Tibagi: a construção do conhecimento sobre os recursos hídricos do Brasil (século XVIII)'. I would like to thank the Biblioteca Brasiliana Mindlin for use of their resources, the librarians, and Cristina Antunes, and also FAPESP for financial support (project 15/21136–3). I am also grateful to Ana Maria de Almeida Camargo for informal conversations about the methodology of History and for providing access to the catalogues of the collections in her personal library.

Transnational Perspectives in Early Twentieth-Century Portugal: The Emergence of the Periodical *Sociedade Futura* (Lisbon, 1902–1904)

Christina Bezari

Ghent University

At the dawn of the twentieth century, editors in Portugal sought to widen the geographic and cultural scope of their publications by incorporating foreign influences and placing their periodicals within a modern European context. A series of considerable changes in their home country, such as the decrease in illiteracy rates, the government's ambitious modernization policies and the subsequent economic growth, encouraged Portuguese editors to look for new ways of expression, to collaborate with their European counterparts and adopt new models of writing and publishing. In many respects, the *fin-de-siècle* period can be considered as the heyday of the Portuguese printed press. As Isabel Soares has shown, editors could benefit from the construction of new telegraph lines, which increased the speed of communications and facilitated contact between Portuguese editors and their correspondents across Europe.[1] This led the national and local press, both daily and weekly, to flourish and to enjoy a greater degree of freedom than it would have in the mid-twentieth century, during the totalitarian Estado Novo regime (1933–74). In this sociocultural context, Ana de Castro Osório (1872–1935) and Maria Olga de Moraes Sarmento da Silveira (1881–1948; referred to here by her married name) started to edit their bimonthly periodical *Sociedade Futura* (1902–04) from their shared office located in the Rua da Glória, in the heart of Lisbon. In order to offer an insight into the editorial agenda of *Sociedade Futura*, as well as to examine its contribution to the public discourse, the present article focuses on the editors' attempts to promote transnational communication and exchange through the periodical. This approach will lead to a better understanding of Castro Osório's and Silveira's editorial practices and will explain the ways in which they envisaged Portugal's place within the European cultural context.

---

[1] Isabel Soares, 'Literary Journalism's Magnetic Pull: Britain's "New" Journalism and the Portuguese at the Fin-de-Siècle', in *Literary Journalism across the Globe: Journalistic Traditions and Transnational Influences*, ed. by John S. Bak and Bill Reynolds (Boston: University of Massachusetts Press, 2011), pp. 118–33 (p. 120).

A number of seminal studies have examined the different aspects of the printed media in Portugal in the late nineteenth and early twentieth centuries, from the development of Portuguese publishing houses and the professionalization of men and women journalists to the role of the press in the creation of feminist associations and movements.[2] These discussions, however, have focused on the figure of the journalist rather than that of the editor. Paula Miranda's analysis of the journalistic experience, for instance, has provided useful insights into prominent journalistic strategies, such as advertising, selling and informing, while Maria Silveirinha's *As mulheres e a afirmação histórica da profissão jornalística* [Women and the historical affirmation of the journalistic profession] has examined the influence of English and American media on Portuguese women journalists.[3] Silveirinha's analysis takes into account the transnational character of the journalistic field by focusing on Portugal's relation to the Anglo-Saxon tradition but does not acknowledge the possibilities that emerge from the interaction between Portugal and the Mediterranean countries. Building on Silveirinha's analysis, this article seeks to elucidate the role of the female periodical editor by focusing on the cultural exchanges that took place between Portugal, Spain and Italy. This approach will allow us to view editors like Castro Osório and Silveira as cultural mediators and agents of social change.

Due to the limited interest in periodicals run by women and owing to its short duration, the periodical *Sociedade Futura* (1902–04) has received little attention from scholars, while the two existing sources on the issue make general statements with regard to its character and objectives. On the one hand, Maria José Remédios posits that it was a feminine periodical that did not serve a feminist agenda; speaking of Castro Osório, she remarks: 'O seu nome vê-se associado à criação, em 1902, da *Sociedade Futura* (publicação feminina sem um índole feminista)' [Her name is associated with the creation, in 1902, of *Sociedade Futura* (a women's publication without a feminist character)].[4] Sofía Sousa Vieira, on the other hand, argues that *Sociedade Futura* forged a positive image of Portuguese women authors who sought to incorporate feminist ideas into their writings: 'Surgen las primeras revistas, tales como *Sociedade Futura* que intentaba ofrecer una imagen positiva de la mujer que intentaba instaurar, a través de sus escritos, una nueva cultura feminista indisolublemente unida a la construcción de la identidad femenina' [There appear the first magazines,

---

[2] Paula Cristina Galvão Mateus Miranda, 'As origens do jornalismo profissional em Portugal: uma incursão pelas estruturas empresariais (1865–1925)', in *Actas do 5º Congresso da Associação Portuguesa de Ciências da Comunicação* (Braga: Centro de Estudos de Comunicação e Sociedade, 2008), pp. 1511–31; Ana Maria Lopes, 'Ousar lutar, ousar vencer: a imprensa periódica oitocentista como motor da promoção intelectual feminina', *Comunicação & Cultura*, 7 (2009), 39–48.
[3] Maria João Silveirinha, 'As mulheres e a afirmação histórica da profissão jornalística: contributos para uma não-ossificação da história do jornalismo', *Comunicação e Sociedade*, 21 (2012), 165–82.
[4] Maria José Remédios, 'Ana de Castro Osório e a construção da Grande Aliança entre os povos: dois manuais da escritora portuguesa adoptados no Brasil', *Faces de Eva. Estudos sobre a Mulher*, 12 (2004), 1–10 (p. 8).

such as *Sociedade Futura*, which aim to offer a positive image of the woman who aims, through her writings, to institute a new feminist culture indissolubly linked to the construction of a feminine identity].[5]

Indeed, both Castro Osório and Silveira dedicated a considerable number of their articles to the life and work of Portuguese and foreign female authors, poets and editors (e.g. Beatriz Pinheiro, Zulmira de Mello, Concepción Gimeno de Flaquer). This decision seems to have been part of a broader feminist initiative to carve out a place for women in the journalistic and literary field. As Celia Carmen Cordeiro has shown, Castro Osório adopted an explicitly feminist discourse at a later period when she became the editor of the periodical *A Semeadora* (Lisbon, 1915–18).[6] Although their later engagement in feminist organizations as well as their respective works *Ás mulheres portuguesas* (1905) and *Mulheres illustres* (1907) are factors to consider when studying the trajectories of Castro Osório and Silveira, the present study takes a different turn, in that it aims to examine the ways in which the two editors perceived and represented *other* cultures in their periodical in order to bring forward the need for social innovation in their home country. Based on this approach, the main questions that will be addressed in this study have to do with the transnational character of *Sociedade Futura* as well as with the way in which it attempted to connect Portugal with southern European countries. More specifically it asks: how did the editors' perception of foreign literature and culture help shape the national identity of early twentieth-century Portugal? How did the two editors aim to make a social impact and which controversial issues were addressed in the periodical? Did salon participation influence editorial strategies and how? By drawing on a range of previously unseen publications and historical sources, as well as through a textual analysis of articles that appeared in *Sociedade Futura*, the present study will give a comprehensive view of Castro Osório's and Silveira's activities as young female editors in Lisbon.

Sociedade Futura under the Tenure of Ana de Castro Osório

A preliminary look into the issues of *Sociedade Futura* that appeared between May 1902 and March 1904 demonstrates that both Castro Osório and Silveira adopted a historical approach to the study of social phenomena. On many occasions, the two women published biographies of illustrious figures and

---

[5] Sofía Sousa Vieira, *Estudio de la actividad musical compositiva y crítica de Francine Benoît* (Salamanca: Ediciones Universidad de Salamanca, 2012), p. 128.

[6] Célia Carmen Cordeiro, 'Semear para colher: a contribuição de Ana de Castro Osório em "A Semeadora" (1915–1918)', in *As mulheres e a imprensa periódica*, ed. by Isabel Lousada and Vania Pinheiro Chaves, 2 vols (Lisbon: CLEPUL, FLUL, 2014), II, 251–65 (p. 253): 'Neste ensaio, darei a conhecer alguns dos ideais que a jornalista feminista semeou e divulgou nas páginas d'*A Semeadora*, nomeadamente o direito das mulheres à educação e ao trabalho remunerado [...]' [In this essay I shall lay out some of the ideas that the feminist journalist planted and spread in the pages of *A Semeadora*, particularly women's right to education and to paid work].

underscored their historical importance and social impact. As Cláudia Pazos Alonso has argued, this practice was already popular among Portuguese female editors of the mid-nineteenth century, such as Francisca Wood (1802–1900).[7] Drawing on previous editorial practices, Castro Osório and Silveira brought historical female figures to the attention of their reading public and highlighted their role as agents of change and arbiters of social values.

Despite its short duration, *Sociedade Futura* went through two different phases. During its first phase, Castro Osório occupied the role of the editor-in-chief (*directora*) while Silveira held the role of the general editor (*redactora*). This administration ended in September 1902, when Silveira became the editor-in-chief and the renowned Portuguese journalist Virgínia Sofia Guerra Quaresma (1882–1973) took on the role of the secretary (*secretária*). From that point Castro Osório took no further part in the journal.

On the front page of the first issue of *Sociedade Futura*, which appeared in May 1902, Castro Osório published a lengthy article on the renowned poet, journalist and *salonnière* Eleonora de Fonseca Pimentel (1752–1799), who was born in Rome to Portuguese noble parents. The following words marked the beginning of Castro Osório's new editorial venture, which aimed to raise awareness of controversial issues such as the role of female editors in the Neapolitan revolution of June 1799:

> Começando a nossa revista por prestar homenagem, sincera e cultual á insigne musa da liberdade napolitana, inscrevendo-a na sua galeria de figuras illustres, como honra do seu sexo, do seu tempo e das duas patrias que a disputam.
>
> [We begin our periodical by paying sincere and devoted homage to the distinguished muse of Neapolitan freedom, recording her in its gallery of illustrious figures, as an honour to her sex, to her time, and to the two countries that dispute her.][8]

By bringing Pimentel's contested nationality to the attention of her readers, Castro Osório uses her as a personification of the cultural links that she wants to draw between Italy and Portugal. This approach provides an interesting lens through which to examine Pimentel's trajectory and, more specifically, her involvement in historical events that shaped the political landscape of late eighteenth-century Italy. According to Castro Osório's article, during the 1790s Pimentel became a member of the Jacobin movement in Naples that aimed to overthrow the Bourbon monarchy and establish a local version of the French Republic. Pimentel's support for the Republican cause and her connections to the Freemasonry seem to have been the main reasons why Castro Osório took an interest in her activities and in her role as a leading figure of the revolution

---

[7] Cláudia Pazos Alonso, 'Modernity in the Making: The Women at the Heart of *A Voz Feminina* and *O Progresso*', in *O feminino e o moderno*, ed. by Ana Luísa Vilela, Flávio Mário Silva and Maria Lúcia dal Farra (Lisbon: CEPUL, 2017), pp. 37–57 (p. 42).
[8] Ana de Castro Osório, 'Leonor da Fonseca Pimentel', *Sociedade Futura*, 1 May 1902, p. 2.

that succeeded in installing a new Republic in January 1799, also known as the Parthenopean Republic. In that year, Pimentel became the editor and the main contributor to the newspaper *Monitore Napoletano* (Naples, 1799), a possible reference to the French *Le Moniteur Universel* (Paris, 1789–1868). When the Republic was overthrown and the Bourbon monarchy was restored, in June 1799, Pimentel was one of the first revolutionaries to be executed by the royal tribunals.

Castro Osório laments her tragic death and praises her obstinate demand for social progress as well as her criticism of religious and political intolerance. This attitude reinforces the subversive tone of the article and places a particular emphasis on the need for a progressive and secular society. In the fight for greater tolerance and freedom of speech, the role of the periodical editor acquires special importance. Castro Osório argues that despite the short duration of the Parthenopean Republic, Pimentel's voice was able to reach a wider public due to the popularity of the press. This in turn raises the question of the low literacy rates, particularly in relation to women, which saw a gradual increase due to the growing influence of the press. It also triggers a reflection on the impact of the Parthenopean Republic on eighteenth-century Naples. Although the outcomes of the revolution were only temporary, Pimentel's influence on public discourse was long-lasting:

> A formosa mulher que foi a alma d'essa ephemera republica, que teve o fugaz destino de tudo quanto é nobre e generoso; a mulher de energias varonis que redigia o *Monitor napolitano*, o jornal official da republica.
>
> [The beautiful woman who was the soul of this ephemeral Republic, which had the fleeting fate of all that is noble and generous; the woman of masculine energy who directed the *Monitore Napoletano*, the official newspaper of the Republic.][9]

In describing her admiration for Pimentel, Castro Osório highlights her belief in the growing power of the press. More than a century after the circulation of the *Monitore Napoletano*, she challenges the values of modern society by pointing to the subversive character of Pimentel's publication and holding it up as exemplary for contemporary and future generations of readers. Castro Osório's interest in Pimentel's newspaper demonstrates the editor's ability to draw on past sources in order to trigger a reflection on the usefulness of cross-cultural encounters. In discussing different styles of periodical editorship, Matthew Philpotts identifies what he calls the 'charismatic mode', based on 'a deeply personalized realization of the editorial role, where the combined capital accumulated by the post-holder is validated largely in their own name and persona', a style that is 'typical of an innovative position in the field'. This style of periodical editorship depends largely on the editor's understanding of historical events and his/her ability to draw on them in order to address

---

[9] Ana de Castro Osório, 'Leonor da Fonseca Pimentel', *Sociedade Futura*, 1 May 1902, p. 2.

contemporary questions.[10] Such a characterization seems quite appropriate for Osório and Silveira. Indeed, by bringing Pimentel to the attention of her public, Castro Osório presents the editor as a visionary figure and an advocate for a fairer society: *uma sociedade futura*. This position suggests that editors can bring real change not only because of their reputation and influence on public discourse but also because of an innate predisposition to do good. This romanticized view of editorship is central in the case of Pimentel, who is represented in the article as the first female editor to have intervened effectively against the monarchy and in favour of the Republic. From this perspective, Castro Osório's homage to Pimentel serves to highlight the objective of her own periodical, which was to engage in cultural transfer and shape the future society, as implied by the title *Sociedade Futura*.

Another question that invites particular consideration has to do with the way in which Castro Osório uses the image of Pimentel to create a link between Portugal and Italy. By mentioning that the two countries are claiming the honour of her origin, she describes a moment of tension but she also creates an open dialogue between cultures and suggests a fruitful crossover between them. In an attempt to bring Pimentel's image closer to her Portuguese readers, she argues that it is their duty to explore 'as relações da heróica musa da republica napolitana, com Portugal, o seu paiz d'origem' [the relations of the heroic muse of the Neapolitan Republic, with Portugal, her country of origin].[11] Through the use of emotional language, Castro Osório stresses the importance of exploring Pimentel's personal trajectory in relation to her cultural background. This exploration leads to the conclusion that, despite its seemingly peripheral position, Portugal entered into dialogue with Italy and enriched its intellectual capital. Castro Osório's intention to remedy Portugal's position is also obvious from the fact that she considers Pimentel's intellectual heritage to be inherently Portuguese, thus creating a tension between the motherland and the society in which she developed her ideas and organized her actions.[12] By creating this tension, Castro Osório raises awareness of Portugal's cultural significance. This does not mean that she dismisses Pimentel's bond with her second country (Italy), but it does, however, suggest that the country of origin (Portugal) maintains a position of power and influence in the processes of cultural production.

Castro Osório's aim to offer a comparative view of Italo-Portuguese relations becomes more concrete in another article on Pimentel, published in the second

---

[10] Matthew Philpotts, 'The Role of the Periodical Editor: Literary Journals and Editorial Habitus', *The Modern Language Review*, 107.1 (2012), 39–64 (p. 48).
[11] Ana de Castro Osório, 'Leonor da Fonseca Pimentel', *Sociedade Futura*, 1 May 1902, p. 1.
[12] Ana de Castro Osório, 'Leonor da Fonseca Pimentel', *Sociedade Futura*, 1 May 1902, p. 1: '[...] Imaginar que os grandes espiritos surgem por milagre, sem raizes na terra, sem filiação na sociedade; isso seria a negação de toda a sciencia e o mais ignaro despreso por todas as regras fataes da hereditariedade e do meio' [To imagine that great spirits emerge by a miracle, without roots in the earth, without a heritage in society; this would be a negation of all science and the most ignorant disdain for all the essential rules of heredity and environment].

issue of *Sociedade Futura* by the Portuguese poet and journalist Joaquim de Araújo (1858–1917). In this article, Araújo advises his audience to read António Cândido de Faria's book *Portugal e Italia*, which describes the trajectory of Portuguese scholars who lived in Italy during the eighteenth century.[13] It is noteworthy, as Araújo emphasizes, that Pimentel's parents had been part of the Portuguese intelligentsia that migrated to Italy in the 1750s. This offers a useful insight into the relations that were forged between the two countries due to the social, cultural and economic impact of immigration in a variety of contexts: interconnection of people and trade flows, cultural representation in literature and in the press, causes and consequences of capital transfer, and changes in the labour market due to people's transnational mobility. Apart from these insights found in Faria's analysis of the relations that developed between Portugal and Italy, Araújo also introduces his audience to Pimentel's play *Il Trionfo della Virtù* (1777), aiming to provide a deeper understanding of her stance towards Portugal: 'Leonor Pimentel, o seu vivo e curioso drama lirico –*Il Trionfo della Virtù*, teve occasião de concorrer no capitulo attinente ás relações que ella criou e manteve com o seu paiz de origem' [In her lively lyrical drama, *Il Trionfo della Virtù*, Leonor Pimentel devoted a chapter to the relations that she created and maintained with her country of origin].[14] In this play, which she dedicated to the Portuguese Prime Minister, the Marquis of Pombal (1699–1782), Pimentel celebrated the abolition of slavery in Portugal and praised the egalitarian policies that limited the prerogatives of the nobility and the clergy. By drawing attention to these historical facts, she constructed a positive image of Portugal and envisioned similar socio-political changes in Italy:

> Ora il Portogallo presta un luminoso esempio di questa verità nel glorioso governo del fedelissimo Giuseppe primo, e nel diligente ministero di V.E.
>
> [Portugal offers a shining example of this truth in the glorious government of the most faithful José the First, and in His Excellency's diligent minister.][15]
>
> Il nome Portoghese passerà alle generazioni future vestito della doppia gloria di avere il primo tratte fra i dubbiosi varchi dell'oceano le nazioni a nuove scoperte, e di aver dato loro l'esempio di regger colla virtù i regni conquistati col valore.
>
> [The Portuguese name will pass on to future generations endowed with the twin glory of being the first to have led nations to new discoveries across the difficult passages of the ocean and to have given them the example of how to rule with virtue and value the realms that they had conquered.][16]

---

[13] Joaquim de Araújo, 'Acerca de Leonor Pimentel', *Sociedade Futura*, 15 May 1902, p. 5: 'Vem no livro do Antonio de Faria — *Portugal e Italia*, na transcripção do jornal *La Sera*'.
[14] Joaquim de Araújo, 'Acerca de Leonor Pimentel', *Sociedade Futura*, 15 May 1902, p. 4.
[15] Eleonora di Fonseca Pimentel, *Il Trionfo della Virtù. Componimento Drammatico* (Naples: n. pub., 1777), p. 32.
[16] Eleonora di Fonseca Pimentel, *Il Trionfo della Virtù*, p. 33.

These excerpts offer useful insights into Pimentel's views on the Portuguese government of the late eighteenth century and its foreign policies. By presenting Portugal as an example to be followed by her Neapolitan compatriots, who sought to overthrow the Bourbon dynasty and declare their own Republic, Pimentel, just like Castro Osório and Araújo, attempted to create a channel of communication between Italy and Portugal. This cross-cultural dialogue transcended national and historical boundaries and was presented as an essential intellectual requirement.

The editor's perception of other countries is, of course, a key element in understanding the importance of this cross-cultural exchange. In the case of Pimentel, for instance, Castro Osório chooses to demonstrate the entanglement of different cultures by creating a tension between the motherland (Portugal) and the country of residence (Italy). This tension does not, however, result in an ideological conflict between the two. On the contrary, it leads to the realization that despite the socio-political differences and the geographical distance between Portugal and Italy, the periodical served as a platform for cultural encounter and exchange. The creation of this platform was Castro Osório's central objective, which she described at the end of her article on Pimentel as a noble endeavour: 'Cumprimos uma parte do nosso programma, cumprindo ao mesmo tempo um gratissimo dever espiritual' [We have fulfilled a part of our programme, fulfilling at the same time a very agreeable spiritual duty].[17] This observation serves as a basis for our analysis of the editorial objectives, the ideas, and the strategies that helped shape the identity of Castro Osório's periodical. As seen thus far, *Sociedade Futura* functioned as an innovative platform advocating for a mutual cultural enrichment between Italy and Portugal and providing a transnational lens through which to consider Portuguese history and culture.

Transnational Perspectives under the Tenure of Maria Olga Sarmento da Silveira

Silveira replaced Castro Osório in September 1902 when she became the editor-in-chief of *Sociedade Futura*. At that time, she was not yet engaged in feminist activism but was known to frequent the artistic salons and bohemian circles of Lisbon. Later on, during the years that she spent in self-imposed exile in Paris (1914–39), she became a member of the *French Astronomical Society*.[18] In her *Mémoires*, Silveira described her life-long relationship with the French Baroness Hélène van Zuylen (1863–1947) and mentioned her 'eterno conflito com as convenções, com os preconceitos portugueses' [never-ending conflict with conventions, with Portuguese prejudices] as the main reason why she left

---

[17] Ana de Castro Osório, 'Leonor da Fonseca Pimentel', *Sociedade Futura*, 1 May 1902, p. 2.
[18] Concepción Núñez Rey, 'Un puente entre España y Portugal: Carmen de Burgos y su amistad con Ana de Castro Osório', *Arbor*, 190.766 (2014), pp. 1–14 (p. 4).

from Portugal at the outbreak of the First World War.[19] As a female editor in her early twenties, Silveira attempted to overcome these prejudices by building bridges with other cultures and familiarizing her Portuguese audience with foreign periodicals and literary works. In this way, she not only continued Castro Osório's cultural mission but also left her mark in the editorial field of early twentieth-century Lisbon.

Throughout her years as an editor, Silveira addressed a wide range of literary and cultural topics, from the emergence of new writers and poets to upcoming events, such as music and dance performances, theatres and salons. A significant part of her contribution to *Sociedade Futura* was to inform the public of the latest literary and journalistic advances outside Portugal, although she dedicated some of her articles to prominent Portuguese authors and feminists, such as Cláudia de Campos (1859–1916) and Alice Moderno (1867–1946).[20] Under her tenure, the editorial objectives of *Sociedade Futura* did not diverge significantly from those that Castro Osório had set, but the tone of the articles did become less polemical and the use of illustrations increased. In many respects, Silveira's perception of foreign cultures influenced her journalistic writings and allowed her to offer a comparative insight into Portugal and Spain. To enrich the literary panorama of her home country, she introduced her audience to Spanish authors such as Concepción Gimeno de Flaquer (1850–1919), Joaquina García Balmaseda (1837–1911) and Carmen de Burgos (1867–1932), and she also shed light on non-canonical literary figures from France such as Maurice Rollinat (1846–1903), Catulle Mendès (1841–1909) and Clémence-Auguste Royer (1830–1902). These are just a few names demonstrating the diversity of foreign literary references that Silveira incorporated into her articles.

Taking into account the possibility of future collaborations with neighbouring Spain, Silveira placed a particular emphasis on women who had built a reputation, not only as writers, but also as journalists and editors of periodicals. In an issue of *Sociedade Futura* that appeared in September 1902, she introduced the Spanish author, editor and salon hostess Gimeno de Flaquer as a transnational influence of particular importance. Although there is nothing to suggest that the two women met in person, Silveira argued in her article that Gimeno de Flaquer's journals *La Ilustración de la Mujer*, *La Cultura Feminina* and particularly her renowned periodical *El Álbum Ibero Americano* had been sources of inspiration for her own journalistic and editorial work.[21]

---

[19] Sarmento da Silveira, *As minhas memórias* (Lisbon: Portugália Editora, 1948), p. 235.
[20] Sarmento da Silveira, 'D. Claudia de Campos', *Sociedade Futura*, 1 November 1902, pp. 1–2 and Maria Olga da Silveira, 'D. Alice Moderno', *Sociedade Futura*, 15 August 1902, pp. 1–2.
[21] Sarmento da Silveira, 'Concepción Gimeno de Flaquer', *Sociedade Futura*, 1 September 1902, p. 1: 'Como jornalista o seu valor è incontestavel. *La Ilustración de la Mujer*, *La Cultura Feminina*, revistas que ella superiormente dirigia, mereceram os mais calorosos applausos do mais selecto meio litterario e scientifico. Actualmente é directora da magnifica revista *El Álbum Ibero Americano* que, com toda a justiça, se pode considerar a par das melhores que se publicam no mundo jornalistico' [Her value as a journalist is incontestable. She has edited the literary journals *La Ilustración de la Mujer* and *La Cultura Feminina*, which deserve the applause of the most prominent literary and scientific circles.

This is an indication that she regarded the periodical as not merely a means of mass production for the distribution of news but rather a living object of aesthetic and intellectual value that could inspire both readers and periodical editors across borders. In her description of Gimeno de Flaquer's career as a periodical editor, Silveira praised her writing style as well as the precision with which she addressed contemporary issues such as the right to education and the intellectual emancipation of women. Although these issues are not treated in detail in Silveira's article, they are represented as ways to increase women's visibility in the literary field. A brief reference to the illustrious figures who invited Gimeno de Flaquer to their salons in Madrid is another way of promoting women's literary and journalistic work. According to a study by Margarita Naharro, Gimeno de Flaquer's own salon was already becoming popular among Portuguese women who sought to disseminate their work abroad. Some examples are the famous poet and journalist Maria Amália Vaz de Carvalho (1847–1921), the editor Guiomar Torrezão (1844–1898), and the novelist Ana Plácido (1831–1895). Naharro argues that these women travelled from Portugal to neighbouring Spain in order to join the salon circles gathered around the famous *salonnière* and benefit from the prestige of potential collaborations with experienced editors.[22] Gimeno de Flaquer's collaboration in Torrezão's periodical *Almanaque das Senhoras* (Lisbon, 1871–98) is an example that illustrates the benefits of salon participation and their echo in the pages of the press.[23] Other examples of transnational co-operations that started from salons can be found in Gimeno de Flaquer's book entitled *En el salón y en el tocador* [In the Salon and at the Dressing Table], published in 1899. In her article, Silveira makes reference to this book, in which female readers could find useful information on the social functions of the Spanish salons, the norms of elite sociability, the art of being elegant, and the importance of eloquence in literary gatherings:

> As obras que escreveu intituladas *La mujer intelectual, En el salón y en el tocador* e muitas produzidas por uma infatigavel e assombrosa perseverancia [...]. A alta sociedade madrilena tem por ella grande sympathia e professa-lhe uma devotada admiração, franqueando-lhe respeitosamente os seus salões.

She is currently the editor of the magnificent *El Álbum Ibero Americano*, which can rightfully be considered as one of the best periodicals in the journalistic world].

[22] Margarita Pintos de Cea-Naharro, *Concepción Gimeno de Flaquer: del sí de las niñas al yo de las mujeres* (Madrid: Plaza y Valdés, 2016), p. 56.

[23] Ana Maria Costa Lopes, *Imagens da mulher na imprensa feminina de oitocentos: percursos de modernidade* (Lisbon: Quimera, 2005), p. 519: 'Em Portugal, a partir dos meados do século XIX observa-se uma acentuada emergência das mulheres na sociedade, sobretudo pelo papel que desempenharam na criação e divulgação de uma imprensa feminina com que intervieram social e culturalmente' [In Portugal, from the middle of the nineteenth century one can see a pronounced emergence of women in society, above all in the role they played in the creation and spread of a feminine press with which they intervened socially and culturally].

[The books that she wrote entitled *La mujer intelectual* [The Intellectual Woman] and *En el salón y en el tocador* [In the Salon and at the Dressing Table] and many [others] produced with a tireless and remarkable perseverance [...]. The high society of Madrid has great regard for her and shows a devoted admiration, respectfully opening up to her its salons.]²⁴

Silveira's allusion to Gimeno de Flaquer's participation in salons in Madrid is noteworthy for two main reasons. Firstly, it brings Portuguese readers closer to a circle of learned women who wished to enhance the circulation of magazines and texts. As Shirley Mangini has observed, salons in Madrid facilitated the dissemination of literary works and allowed erudite women to become the 'authentic chroniclers' of their time.²⁵ Secondly, Silveira's article illustrates the strong connections that were developed between the culture produced by salon life and the one promoted on a larger scale by the print industry. To examine the complementary roles of female editors and *salonnières*, it is necessary to look into the ways in which Gimeno de Flaquer's participation is represented in Silveira's article. Madrid society's admiration for her is a central element. Silveira deliberately establishes a hierarchical relation between them in order to highlight the hostess's privileged position as an arbiter of intellectual debate. This helps the reader perceive the salon not merely as a space for exchange and dialogue but also as a prestigious forum, offering the opportunity to become part of a transnational cultural network of writers, journalists and editors who gathered around the charismatic figure of the *salonnière*. Whether motivated by the idea of meeting Gimeno de Flaquer in a salon, or by the possibility of making new contacts within the literary circles of Madrid, Silveira draws a parallel between salon activities and periodical editorship. The dynamic combination of these fields is crucial because it advances our understanding of women's editorial practices and paves the way for a more comprehensive study of their private and public initiatives.

Whether under the editorship of Castro Osório or under Silveira, *Sociedade Futura* promoted the example of foreign women such as Pimentel and Gimeno de Flaquer, both of whom were leading figures in the editorial field and in the salon circles of their time. By bringing these examples to the attention of their public, the two editors of *Sociedade Futura* engaged in the task of deciphering other cultures, hence situating themselves on cultural, political and linguistic boundaries. Their articles bear witness to the connections that existed between Portugal, Spain and Italy and reflect the growing complexity of these relations at a time in which the wider public viewed women's influence as limited in scope or restricted to the domestic sphere. This conservative view of women's role in society was also enhanced by the Catholic Church, which, as Deborah

---

²⁴ Sarmento da Silveira, 'Concepción Gimeno de Flaquer', *Sociedade Futura*, 1 September 1902, p. 1.
²⁵ Shirley Mangini, *Las modernas de Madrid: las grandes intelectuales españolas de la vanguardia* (Madrid: Península, 2001), p. 151: '[...] mujeres como auténticas cronistas de la situación de la intelectual moderna' [women as authentic chroniclers of the situation of the modern female intellectual].

Madden has shown, opposed women's right to vote during the first decades of the twentieth century.[26] To counterbalance the power of the Church, female editors saw literary translation as a way to enhance the circulation of women's works across national boundaries and to strengthen the periodical's position between cultural and linguistic traditions. To facilitate the reception of foreign female writers in Portugal, Silveira included in the pages of *Sociedade Futura* a permanent column dedicated to translations of literary texts. One remarkable example is Vittoria Colonna's poem *Canzoniere*, translated from Italian into French by the Baroness de Tallenay; this choice suggests that most lusophone readers would be conversant with French. Another translation that appeared in this column was Carmen de Burgos's poem *Cantares*, which was translated from Spanish into Portuguese by Silveira herself.[27] These examples point to the plurality of cultural references that Silveira promoted through the pages of her periodical. They also attest to the transnational character of *Sociedade Futura* and to Silveira's role as a mediator between cultures.

Along with their position as periodical editors, both Castro Osório and Silveira welcomed foreign attendees in the literary salons that they held in Lisbon.[28] Their double role as editors and salon hostesses is a practice that requires closer scrutiny because it helped them to enhance the circulation of foreign literature in the Portuguese market. In fact, representational strategies that editors used to promote the work of their foreign friends to the public functioned as the basis of a social network that developed in private salons. This observation is key to understanding representation as a major editorial technique aiming to increase consumption. From this perspective, the work of foreign salon attendees such as the Spanish Carmen de Burgos, the Brazilian Lucinda Simões, and the French Marie-Louise Néron was represented in the pages of *Sociedade Futura* in order to increase their visibility in the public sphere. This editorial practice leads to the conclusion that the modern salon complemented the periodical in its effort to boost interactions between cultures. Salon participation also allowed women to meet with editors who could potentially help them to publish their work and make a name for themselves. In light of this analysis, Silveira's mediation, either through her periodical or through her salon, had a cultural purpose but also aimed to serve her social status and financial interests.

João Esteves and Zília Osório de Castro highlight the importance of salon gatherings in defining the content and the main objectives of a periodical.[29] Their study shows that prominent female journalists such as Maria Veleda

---

[26] Deborah Madden, 'Historical Context in Portugal', in *A New History of Iberian Feminisms*, ed. by Silvia Bermúdez and Roberta Johnson (Toronto: University of Toronto Press, 2018), p. 201.

[27] Vittoria Colonna, 'Cancioneiro Estrangeiro', trans. by the Baroness de Tallenay, *Sociedade Futura*, 1 November 1902, p. 2 and Carmen de Burgos, 'Cantares', *Sociedade Futura*, 1 May 1903, p. 2.

[28] João Esteves, 'Dos salões literários ao associativismo pacifista, feminista, maçónico, republicano e socialista'. Online source: <http://lagosdarepublica.wikidot.com/associativismopacifista> [accessed 6 July 2018].

[29] Zília Osório de Castro and João Esteves, *Feminae: dicionário contemporâneo* (Lisbon: Comissão para a Cidadania e a Igualdade de Género, 2013), pp. 522–23.

(1871–1955) and the secretary of *Sociedade Futura*, Virgínia Quaresma, gathered in Silveira's salon to discuss the topics that they would address in their forthcoming articles. The discussions could sometimes lead to disagreements about the ideological stance of the periodical or about the material that was to be published. It is worth noting that Veleda criticized Quaresma's contributions to *Sociedade Futura* as well as to the *Jornal da Mulher*, a women's supplement to the newspaper *O Mundo*, which she viewed as conservative. In her opinion, editors who addressed a predominantly female audience needed to advocate for women's rights instead of merely promoting recipes, fashion, embroidery, poetry and short stories. Veleda's critical view of the material that appeared in *Sociedade Futura* brought her into conflict with Silveira and Quaresma, who adopted a less militant approach. The setting of this conflict was the literary salon, which served as a forum for discussion and decision-making. Despite Veleda's objections, Silveira's and Quaresma's articles focused on literature and culture rather than political and feminist movements. The transnational approach that they adopted in the study of literature helped them to define the content of *Sociedade Futura* and to offer new material and reading experiences to their audience.

As the discussion thus far has demonstrated, many of the articles that appeared in *Sociedade Futura* attempted to import foreign literature into Portugal. This was a way to facilitate dialogue across borders and to attract the reader's attention to the journalistic and literary production of that period. Nevertheless, a number of the articles that Silveira edited also functioned as points of departure for self-reflection and social critique. To accomplish this goal, Silveira gave voice to foreign visitors and scholars who drew attention to processes of social progress in Portugal. One remarkable example is the renowned British historian Edgar Prestage (1869–1951), who provided an article entitled 'Portugal visto por um extrangeiro' [Portugal Seen by a Foreigner], in which he emphasized the natural beauty of the country but pointed to an urgent need for social innovation. This critical approach to the socio-political landscape of Portugal highlighted the inefficiency of austerity measures, the royal family's expenses, and the importance of transparency in public affairs: 'Falta-lhe sómente uma boa administração, a qual conseguiria mais do que todas as medidas repressivas' [She lacks only a good administration, which could achieve more than all the repressive measures].[30] This passage alludes to the instability of the two political parties (*Progressivo* and *Regenerador*) as well as to a number of socio-political events that destabilized Portugal and created a sense of pessimism during the last decade of the nineteenth century, in particular the British pressure on the Portuguese government, also known as the 1890 British Ultimatum, which forced the retreat of Portuguese military forces from Britain's African colonies.

---

[30] Edgar Prestage, 'Portugal visto por um extrangeiro', *Sociedade Futura*, 15 December 1902, p. 1.

On a more positive note, Prestage stressed the role of literature in overcoming tensions and bringing change to society: 'para fazer recuar a onda de pessimismo que se tem alastrado pelo paiz, e que tem sido a nota predominante da litteratura, nos ultimos quarenta annos' [to push back the wave of pessimism that has spread throughout the country, and which has been the predominant note in literature over the last forty years].[31] Although there are no specific examples of authors mentioned in this article, Prestage underscored the value of literature as a means to confront the moral crisis and to provoke a shift in the socio-cultural panorama of early twentieth-century Portugal. This stance reveals some of the goals that Silveira set for her periodical. Her publications aimed to induce social change by promoting Portugal's need for political stability and by advancing literature and art as means to overcome national pessimism. They also aimed to intervene at the cultural level by encouraging Portuguese writers and readers to accept and incorporate foreign influences. Finally, Silveira's publications adopted a transnational perspective by introducing Portugal as a legitimate cultural centre capable of participating in the ongoing exchanges between European nations.

Following Prestage's example, Silveira published an article in May 1903, in which she discussed an alarming sense of pessimism felt among the educated elite concerning Portugal's sense: 'Como a Allemanha no tempo de Schubert, tambem Portugal atravessa agora uma crise depressiva, e para levantar o genio nacional é preciso communicar-lhe a consciencia da sua individualidade ethnica e historica' [Like Germany at the time of Schubert, Portugal too is now undergoing a crisis of depression, and in order to raise the national spirit it is necessary to communicate to her an awareness of her ethnic and historical individuality].[32] By way of comparison, Silveira addressed the moral crisis that disillusioned the most prominent literary figures of the *Geração de setenta*, namely Eça de Queiroz and Oliveira Martins. According to her analysis, this moment of crisis was manifested due to a growing desire among the Europeanized elite to restore the power and glory that Portugal enjoyed during the Age of the Discoveries (1415–1550). As Douglas Wheeler and Walter Opello have argued, the *Geração de setenta* sought to criticize the pervasive feeling of decadence and called for reform and renewal.[33] Drawing on these ideas, Silveira, just like Castro Osório, aspired to play a role in raising the public's awareness of Portugal's historical position and identity. To achieve this objective, they both felt the need to bring Portugal into dialogue with other cultures instead of choosing isolation or a vain glorification of the past. This is the key to understanding some of their editorial choices as well as the position

---

[31] Ibid.
[32] Sarmento da Silveira, 'Fragmento d'um Programma Musical', *Sociedade Futura*, 1 May 1903, p. 1.
[33] Douglas Wheeler and Walter Opello, *Historical Dictionary of Portugal* (Lanham, MD: Scarecrow Press, 2010), p. 144: 'Like so many other movements in modern Portugal, the Generation of 1870's initiatives began essentially as a protest by university students of Coimbra, who confronted the status quo and sought to change their world by means of innovation in action and ideas'.

of *Sociedade Futura* in the socio-cultural landscape of early twentieth-century Portugal.

Conclusion

In retrospect, Silveira's and Castro Osório's editorial venture was part of a broader strategy to encourage the consolidation of a national identity through a solid knowledge of other cultural realities and worldviews. The parallels that they established between Portuguese and foreign women poets, writers and salon attendees are an essential part of their contribution to *Sociedade Futura*. The reason for this is that such parallels enhanced the readers' knowledge of other European realities and reinforced Portugal's position in the intellectual debate of the time. Nevertheless, as Kyra Giorgi has observed, a concern that arose at the end of the nineteenth century had to do with Portugal's seemingly peripheral position within the broader cultural landscape.[34] Indeed, the anxiety at being on the fringes caused a deep-rooted pessimism, which was highlighted in our analysis of Prestage's article. Silveira's response to this feeling of pessimism was to reconstruct a national identity on the basis of transnational dialogue and exchange. For this reason, both her publications and her salon in Lisbon functioned as cultural forums favouring transnational communication and creating collaborative opportunities. In the same way as the parallel feminist movements of the time, the numerous collaborations in magazines and periodicals brought together female intellectuals from different parts of Europe. Nonetheless, in an article that appeared in March 1904, Silveira expressed a particular preference for the so-called *mulheres de raza latina* [women of Latin origins] such as Gimeno de Flaquer: 'Comquanto não seja uma obra portugueza, não deixa por isso de grangear a nossa sympathia e de motivar, para nos, sincero prazer intellectual mais esta manifestação do fecundo talento de Gimeno de Flaquer' [Although it is not a Portuguese work, this further manifestation of the fecund talent of Gimeno de Flaquer does not fail to gain our sympathy and to occasion, for us, sincere intellectual pleasure].[35] Either as a strategic move aiming to unify women from southern Europe or merely as a way to highlight their importance, this article demonstrates Silveira's attempt to create a sense of belonging by including Portugal in the broader context of the Latin-rooted countries of Europe.[36] This move sheds light on a significant aspect of her editorial policy, which ultimately aimed to bring Portugal closer to its Latin heritage.

Despite its transnational scope and rich content, *Sociedade Futura* was not able to secure a strong market position and ceased to exist in March 1904. In

---

[34] See Kyra Giorgi, *Emotions, Language and Identity on the Margins of Europe* (London: Palgrave Macmillan, 2014), p. 48: 'Although peripherality is sometimes subjective, it rarely arises solely from the imagination; a sense of outsiderness is usually grounded in very real experiences of loss, exclusion and deprivation'.
[35] Sarmento da Silveira, 'Mulheres de raza latina', *Sociedade Futura*, 1 March 1904, p. 64.
[36] Her sense of belonging seems to be more oriented towards Spain, Italy, and France.

the final issue, Silveira published an article on the Romanian poet Lucile Kitzô (1873–?). The article was followed by two sonnets that Kitzô had dedicated to the second President of Portugal, Teófilo Braga (1843–1924) and his spouse. In her article, Silveira viewed the Romanian tradition and culture as essentially Latin and created a parallel between Romania and Portugal.[37] According to her analysis, although both countries had been inclined to incorporate Western influences in order to escape their peripheral position, they did, however, maintain their Latin roots, which were obvious above all in their languages.[38] From this perspective, Silveira placed Portugal alongside Romania and highlighted that their geographical position, either on the outskirts of Europe or among Slavic nations, did not obscure their Latin identity. This argument reflects an acute perception of Portugal's cultural heritage and explains the editor's ambition to act as a mediator between countries and cultures. In light of this analysis, Castro Osório's and Silveira's periodical *Sociedade Futura* can be seen as a vital first step towards defining Portugal's cultural position within the broader European landscape. Their numerous collaborations with foreign journals such as the Spanish *Revista Crítica* and the French *Mercure de France*, as well as their assiduous participation in the salons of influential women journalists in Lisbon, Paris and Madrid, including Alice Moderno, Lucie Delarue-Mardrus and Carmen de Burgos, are factors that increased their impact in Portugal and beyond.[39]

---

[37] Sarmento da Silveira, 'Lucile Kitzô', *Sociedade Futura*, 1 March 1904, p. 54.
[38] Both Portuguese and Romanian are Romance languages. They are also known as Latin or Neo-Latin languages.
[39] For more information on Silveira's activities in Paris see Fernando Curopos, 'Les Mémoires de Maria Olga Morais de Sarmento: discours public, amours secrètes', *Inverses*, 11 (2011), 23–32.

Hybridity and Prejudice: Jews and New Christians in *Casa-Grande & Senzala* and the Intellectual Context of Gilberto Freyre

CLAUDE B. STUCZYNSKI

Bar-Ilan University, Ramat-Gan

1

In 1933, Gilberto de Mello Freyre (1900–1987) revolutionized historiography with his masterwork *Casa-Grande & Senzala* ('Masters and Slaves'). The author described his book as a 'Proustian introspection' about everyday dealings between masters and slaves on the sugar plantations of Northeastern colonial Brazil. Freyre conceived that his 'social history of the Big House [Casa Grande] is the intimate history of practically every Brazilian: the history of his domestic and conjugal life under a slave-holding and polygamous patriarchal regime; the history of his life as a child; the history of his Christianity, reduced to the form of a family religion and influenced by the superstitions of the slave hut [Senzala]'. He considered this approach closer to 'the being of a people' and more accurate and meaningful than the pompous and misleading official narratives of political and military heroic feats (p. xliii).[1] In this respect, Freyre was in line with the founders of the French *Annales* school, Marc Bloch (1866–1944) and Lucien Febvre (1878–1956), who introduced deep, totalizing studies of the past that were supported by the social sciences.[2] Nevertheless, Freyre's work was pioneering, displaying a fusion of his skills as a bohemian journalist and his studies with the German-American anthropologist Franz Boas (1858–1942).[3]

Freyre offered a sociological, anthropological and historical reading of Brazil that generates reverence and controversy to this day. Alternately incisive and arbitrary, profound and superficial, iconoclastic and biased, the

---

[1] Throughout this article, the pagination of *Casa-Grande & Senzala* will follow the second English edition of Freyre's book (Gilberto Freyre, *The Masters and the Slaves [Casa-Grande & Senzala]: A Study in the Development of Brazilian Civilization*, trans. from the Portuguese by Samuel Putnam, revd edn (New York: Alfred A. Knopf, 1956).
[2] Peter Burke, 'Gilberto Freyre e a Nova História', *Tempo Social*, 9.2 (1997), 1–12.
[3] Enrique Rodríguez Larreta and Guillermo Giucci, *Gilberto Freyre: uma biografia cultural: a formação de um intelectual brasileiro, 1900–1936* (Rio de Janeiro: Civilização Brasileira, 2007), esp. pp. 137–42, 451–60; Maria Pallares-Burke, *Gilberto Freyre: um vitoriano dos trópicos* (São Paulo: UNESP, 2005), chap. 3.

impressionistic and singular character of *Casa-Grande & Senzala* made the book a fundamental reference point for discussions about the past and future of Brazil. Freyre proposed a novel national narrative in which the genesis of Brazil's quintessence (*brasilidade*, 'Brazilianness') was located in the interaction between the Portuguese plantation master and his African slaves. Rejecting dominant Eurocentric historical narratives and 'whitening' policies promoted by the government and the elites, Freyre identified racial miscegenation and cultural hybridization between masters and slaves as foundational in the formation of an enduring patriarchal system. Thus, he was among the first historians to situate blacks as leading elements in the crafting of Brazil's collective identity, elevating them from a minor historiographical role as a socioculturally marginalized workforce.[4]

In actuality, what Freyre portrayed as an intimate Brazil — which one could also call promiscuous — was never a simple encounter between the dominating 'white race' and the dominated 'black race'. Beyond the recognition of the influence of indigenous groups (especially during the initial phases of exploration and settlement and in the regions under the influence of the *bandeirantes*) and the ethnic and cultural diversity of groups of African slaves in Brazil, Freyre argued that the Portuguese settlers brought with them a long tradition of previous hybridizations and miscegenations. The history of Portugal, Freyre contended, incorporated traces left by Celts, Phoenicians, Latins, Germans, Arabs, Africans and Jews. He described the Portuguese people as 'existing indeterminately between Europe and Africa and belonging uncompromisingly to neither one nor the other of the two continents', with this racial indeterminacy explaining the nation's oscillations between energy and apathy (p. 4). For Freyre, this 'mestizo heritage' accounted for the easy adaptation of the Portuguese settlers to the new colonial reality. In fact, Freyre held that his native country exemplified what he would later term 'Luso-tropicalism': a model of imperial integration of indigenous peoples and miscegenation between colonizers and colonized that was more inclusive than other European projects of colonial expansion.[5]

---

[4] Thomas E. Skidmore, *Preto no branco: raça e nacionalidade no pensamento brasileiro* (Rio de Janeiro: Editora Paz e Terra, 1976); Sérgio Miceli, *Intelectuais e classe dirigente no Brasil (1920-1925)* (São Paulo: Difel, 1979); Edson Nery da Fonseca (ed.), *Casa-Grande & Senzala e a crítica brasileira de 1933 a 1944* (Recife: Companhia Editora de Pernambuco, 1985); Lilia Moritz Schwarcz, *O espetáculo das raças: cientistas, instituições e questão racial no Brasil, 1870-1930* (São Paulo: Companhia das Letras, 1993); Manuel Correia de Andrade, 'Gilberto Freyre e o impacto dos anos 30', *Revista USP*, 38 (1998), 38–47; David Clarey, 'Race, Nationalism and Social Theory in Brazil: Rethinking Gilberto Freyre', *David Rockefeller Center for Latin American Studies* (Cambridge, MA: Harvard University, 1999); Maria Alice Rezende de Carvalho, '*Casa-Grande & Senzala* e o pensamento social brasileiro', in Gilberto Freyre, *Casa-Grande & Senzala*, ed. by Guillermo Giucci, Enrique Rodríguez Larreta and Edson Nery da Fonseca (Paris: ALLCA, 2002), pp. 877–908.

[5] Gilberto Freyre, *Conferencias na Europa* (Rio de Janeiro: Ministério de Educação e Saúde, 1938), p. 14; idem, *O Luso e o Trópico: sugestões em torno dos métodos portugueses de integração de povos autóctones e de culturas diferentes da europeia num complexo novo de civilização: o Luso-Tropical* (Lisbon: Comissão executiva das comemorações do V centenário da morte do infante D. Henrique, 1961).

After analysing the formation of patriarchal society in *Casa-Grande & Senzala*, Freyre continued his investigation in 1936 with *Sobrados e Mucambos* ('Mansions and Shanties'), studying the further development of this society during the disappearance of the slave-owning regime. In *Ordem e Progresso* ('Order and Progress'), published in 1957, he completed his trilogy on Brazil's patriarchal society by identifying its last traces in the first days of the Republic of 1889. Thus, in a radical move, Freyre inverted the dominant criticism made by Euclides da Cunha (1866–1909), who had identified racial miscegenation in Brazil as a 'decadent' process that led to the creation of an alternative but inauthentic 'loan culture' of European origin. Together with Latin American thinkers of his generation, such as the Mexican politician and thinker José Vasconcelos Calderón (1881–1959), Freyre was instrumental in the creation of an abiding mythical image of Latin America as a paradise for the mulatto and the mestizo.[6] It is true that Freyre's political proclivities — shifting from regionalist, nationalist to conservative — accorded well with the new governmental policies of 'carnavalization' of Brazilian culture during the anti-democratic period led by Getúlio Vargas (1930–45).[7] Nevertheless, from the contemporary vantage point of an uncertain globalization witnessing real and imaginary 'clashes of civilizations', *Casa-Grande & Senzala* could be easily regarded as a progressive manifesto that celebrates a multi-racial and mestizo worldview: antidotes to xenophobia and racism, anywhere and anytime.[8]

2

Taking the above into account, it is easy to understand why some readers were surprised by the way Freyre discussed Judaism, Jews, and New Christians (conversos) in *Casa-Grande & Senzala*, articulating stereotypes such as their 'natural propensity' for commerce and usury, their purported disdain for working the land and for other productive labour, and their alleged love of exhibitionist intellectuality. In a notorious passage omitted from the English translation of the book, Freyre outlined a sketch of Jews that seemed to come from the worst anti-Semitic caricatures of those times: '[i]n this way, Jews became almost everywhere technicians of usury through an almost biological

---

[6] Euclides da Cunha, 'Os Sertões', in *Obras Completas* (Rio de Janeiro: Aguilar, 1966), II, 168.
[7] Ricardo Benzaquén de Araújo, *Guerra e Paz: Casa-Grande & Senzala e a obra de Gilberto Freyre nos anos 30*, 2nd edn (São Paulo: Ed. 34, 2005), esp. pp. 183–207; Alexandra Isfahani-Hammond (ed.), *The Masters and the Slaves: Plantation Relations and Mestizaje in American Imaginaries* (New York: Palgrave Macmillan, 2005).
[8] Stuart B. Schwartz, 'Gilberto Freyre e a história colonial: uma visão otimista do Brasil', in Freyre, *Casa-Grande & Senzala*, ed. by Guillermo Giucci, Enrique Rodríguez Larreta and Edson Nery da Fonseca, pp. 909–21. For critical approaches to Freyre's purported progressive hybridism, see Cláudia Castelo, 'Uma incursão no lusotropicalismo de Gilberto Freyre', in *bHL-blogue de História Lusófona*, Ano VI (2011), pp. 261–80; Miguel Vale de Almeida, *An Earth-colored Sea: 'Race', Culture and the Politics of Identity in the Post-Colonial Portuguese-Speaking World* (New York: Berghahn, 2005), pp. 45–64.

process of specialization, which seems to have sharpened their profiles like birds of prey, their gestures with constant expressions of acquisition and possession, turning their hands into claws incapable of sowing and breeding. Only capable of hoarding'.[9] Furthermore, in order to show the supposedly corrosive influence of Judaism, Freyre coined two terms: '*israelitamente*', denoting a greedily obsessive manner of doing commerce — a neologism replaced in the English translation by 'in the manner of the Israelites' (p. 33) — and '*sefardínicas*', referring to the use of the image of intellectualism as a manner of acquiring social distinction, purportedly applied by the Jews of the Iberian Peninsula, or *Sepharad* — translated as 'their Sephardic traditions of intellectuality' (p. 232).[10] Thus, when prefacing *Casa-Grande & Senzala* in the Spanish translation included in the prestigious Venezuelan 'Biblioteca Ayacucho', sociologist Darcy Ribeiro (1922–1997) expressed his dismay at such stereotypes voiced by an apologist for human diversity. Recalling the sympathy Freyre expressed towards Muslim and Black influences, Ribeiro wrote that 'concerning the Jew, on the contrary, the portrait is grotesque and merciless'.[11]

It was the American anthropologist Jules Henry (1904–1969), however, a scholar of the indigenous Latin-American cultures and a disciple of Boas, who, in 1947, levelled strong criticism at *Casa-Grande & Senzala* in a review of the book's translation into English under the title *Masters and Slaves* (1946). Henry began by applauding Freyre's unbiased description of Afro-Brazilians, as well as his intriguing account of the centrality of miscegenation in Brazil. It did not take long, however, before he opened fire on Freyre's caricature of indigenous peoples as effeminate and awkward and, above all, his 'less than charitable' attitude towards Jews and 'the history of these unfortunate people'. According to Henry, Freyre failed to mention that the alleged propensity of Jews for commercial activities and usury had been imposed by a hostile environment or the falsity of the claim that Jews had introduced slavery to Portugal: '[a]n enemy of manual toil, the Jew from remote times had a bent toward slavery [...] [a]nd certain it is that many Jews in the peninsula, from a time beyond that of which we have record, were the owners of Christian slaves and possessed Christian concubines' (p. 232). Henry pointed to Freyre's unscientific prejudices, relying on the anti-Semitic racism of one of the ideologues of Nazism: Houston Stewart

---

[9] 'Técnicos da usura, tais se tornaram os judeus em quase toda parte por um processo de especialização quase biológica que lhes parece ter aguçado o perfil no de ave de rapina, a mímica em constantes gestos de aquisição e de posse, as mãos em garras incapazes de semear e de criar. Capazes só de amealhar' (Freyre, *Casa-Grande & Senzala. Formação da família brasileira sob o regime da economia patriarcal*, op. cit., p. 305). This omission was probably the initiative of Samuel Putnam, the English translator of *Casa-Grande & Senzala* (Freyre, *The Masters and the Slaves [Casa-Grande & Senzala]. A Study in the Development of Brazilian Civilization*, op. cit., p. 230, n. 105). As we shall see, a similar apologetic response will be given by Freyre himself against his detractors in ulterior editions of the book.
[10] Cf. Freyre, *Casa-Grande & Senzala. Formação da família brasileira sob o regime da economia patriarcal*, pp. 86, 307.
[11] Darcy Ribeiro, 'Prólogo', in Gilberto Freyre, *Casa-Grande y Senzala* (Caracas: Biblioteca Ayacucho, 1977), p. xxix.

Chamberlain (1855–1927). Thus, for Henry, *Casa-Grande & Senzala* was an imprecise and useless book for the study of historical anthropology and he lamented that such work, published in the 'prophetic year' of 1933 (i.e. Hitler's ascension to power in Germany), had been now translated into English: 'it is unfortunate that a work of this sort is unleashed upon a world already seething with race hatred'.[12]

Such views have led some contemporary scholars to identify an anti-Semitic discourse in Freyre's works, something that was particularly evident in *Casa-Grande & Senzala* but had already been manifested in the first journalistic pieces of his youth, and would appear in his later works, especially in *Sobrados e Mucambos*.[13] This discourse can be explained by his premature adhesion to anti-Semitic conservative ideologies and prejudices that circulated in Brazil and abroad, for instance in the work of Maurice Barrès (1862–1923) and Charles Maurras (1868–1952) of *l'Action Française*.[14] It is true that in *Casa-Grande & Senzala* these biases were articulated through the citation of Chamberlain's *Die Grundlagen des neunzehnten Jahrhunderts* (1889) in its English translation (pp. 79, 232). One can also glimpse a simplistic adoption of the theses of the authoritative German sociologist Max Weber (1864–1920) in his *Das antike Judentum*, which argued that the Mosaic religion had created a system of double morality ('doppelte Moral') that distinguished between rigid norms among members of the Jewish religion and more lax ethical principles when dealing with gentiles (p. 230). As we shall see, some of these ideas originated with the man Freyre saw as his main mentor in matters of Portugal's economic history and its Jewish and New Christian or converso communities, the Portuguese historian João Lúcio de Azevedo (1855–1933). Specifically, one may mention here the thesis of the anti-Jewish economic historian Werner Sombart (1863–1941) that there was a causal link between Jewish religion and capitalism understood as a reified accumulation of riches.[15] On the pages of *Casa-Grande & Senzala*, Jews appear associated with an alienating materialism that promotes a social isolationism, something which 'naturally' provokes rejection and hostility on the part of the rest of the nations. Thus, the unexpected treatment of Jews and New Christians in a book which celebrates human difference is the result of perceiving the former as exceptionally negative.

Significantly, this impression was shared neither by the author of *Casa-Grande & Senzala* nor by the majority of its critics. In the preface to the sixth Portuguese edition (1950), Freyre explicitly denied such accusations. In his

---

[12] Jules Henry, 'Review of "The Masters and the Slaves"', *American Journal of Orthopsychiatry*, 17 (1947), 730–32.

[13] Júlio José Chiavenato, *O inimigo eleito: os Judeus, o poder e o anti-Semitismo* (Porto Alegre: Mercado Aberto, 1985), pp. 268–72; Silvia Cortez Silva, 'O discurso anti-Semita na obra de Gilberto Freyre', in *O anti-Semitismo nas Américas*, ed. by Maria Luiza Tucci Carneiro (São Paulo: EDUSP, 2007), pp. 323–50; idem, *Tempos de Casa-Grande (1930–1940)* (São Paulo: Perspectiva, 2010), esp. pp. 63–96.

[14] Larreta & Giucci, *Gilberto Freyre*, pp. 170–75.

[15] On the influence of Sombart in Azevedo's work, see, for instance João Lúcio de Azevedo, *História dos Cristãos-Novos Portugueses* (Lisbon: Clássica Editora, 1989), pp. 33–34.

view, although he never had the negative disposition towards Jews that Henry attributed to him, he did not stand for 'an idealized view' of them either. He also claimed that Henry's review suffered from the very lack of scientific balance that his critic had accused *Casa-Grande & Senzala* of. For Henry, 'wishes to grant to the Jews a treatment other than the somehow irreverent one my book grants the Spaniards, the English, the Portuguese, the indigenous groups, the mestizos and Brazilians themselves. A preferential treatment that consists of a so vehement reaction to anti-Semitism, as to become sheer apologetic pro-Semitism'.[16] In a bibliographical dossier on the reception of *Casa-Grande & Senzala* in Brazil and abroad, prepared by Guillermo Giucci and Enrique Rodríguez Larreta (2002), the 'Jewish Question' does not appear at all as a relevant topic raised in the numerous reviews and articles dedicated to the book.[17]

All things considered, I believe that a specific animosity towards Jews, Judaism, and New Christians in *Casa-Grande & Senzala* is undeniable, particularly when compared to the more 'irreverent' sympathy Freyre showed to other groups. According to Silvia Cortez Silva, Freyre 'neatly disagreed only once with the ideas of anti-Semitic authors', when in *Sobrados e Mucambos* he rejected Azevedo's objection to Sombart's view that 'the cultivation of sugarcane and processing of sugar in Brazil had been an accomplishment of Jews'.[18] Actually, in *Sobrados e Mucambos*, Freyre recommended caution in dismissing Sombart's assertion and accepting that of Azevedo before more systematic studies on Brazil's sugar industry were made.[19] Basing himself on a proverbial Jewish solidarity and economic specialization, Freyre proposed to differentiate between what he outlined as the 'middleman' role of the 'Jews' (i.e. the New Christians) as slave merchants, traders and merchants and the 'creative grandeur' of the Portuguese sugar planter. For Freyre, while it was true that the former lived 'in the shadow of the patriarchal Portuguese', we should not attribute to them a mere 'parasitic' function, since '[w]ithout the Jewish moneylender, it is almost certain that Brazil would not have acquired such a swift and complete monopoly of the European sugar market so that the output of the plantations of Pernambuco, Itamaracá and Paraíba at the beginning of the seventeenth century yielded more revenue to the Crown than the entire trade of India with all the glitter of its rubies and rustle of silks'.[20] That being said, neither in *Casa-Grande & Senzala* nor in any other of Freyre's writings

---

[16] Gilberto Freyre, *Casa-Grande & Senzala. Formação da família brasileira sob o regime da economia patriarcal* (Rio de Janeiro: Livraria José Olympio Editora, 1954), pp. 84–86.
[17] Freyre, *Casa-Grande & Senzala*, ed. by Guillermo Giucci, Enrique Rodríguez Larreta and Edson Nery da Fonseca, op. cit., pp. 923–1135.
[18] Cortez Silva, 'O discurso anti-Semita na obra de Gilberto Freyre', p. 327 n. 12; idem, *Tempos de Casa-Grande (1930–1940)*, p. 89. Cf. João Lúcio de Azevedo, *Épocas de Portugal económico: esboços de história* (Lisbon: Livraria Clássica Editora, 1929), p. 264.
[19] Gilberto Freyre, *The Mansions and the Shanties [Sobrados e Mucambos]: The Making of Modern Brazil*, trans. and ed. by Harriet de Onís, with an intro. by Frank Tannenbaum (New York: Alfred A. Knopf, 1963), pp. 11–12.
[20] Ibid, p. 13.

does one encounter such a neat ethno-functional differentiation, since the sugar industry was depicted as the outcome of a 'Semitic' know-how.

Nevertheless, it seems to me that Júlio José Chiavenato overstated the case in his claim that more harm was done by the 'subtle' and 'intelligent' anti-Semitic discourse of the authoritative and respectful Freyre than by the 'fanatic' promoter of the 'Protocols of Zion' in Brazil, Gustavo Barroso (1888–1957).[21] Moreover, I disagree with Cortez Silva's claim that: 'in spite of presenting the Portuguese as an Iberian amalgam in which there was a Jewish element, Freyre insisted in excluding the latter from the formation of Brazil'.[22] I argue that both Chiavenato and Cortez Silva failed to see that alongside his strongly negative stereotypes, Freyre celebrated the adaptability, entrepreneurial spirit, and intellectual curiosity of Jews and New Christians. For instance, he claimed that one of the constitutive elements of Brazil's nationhood was 'Semitic' mobility and adaptability, qualities that 'are easily to be made out in the Portuguese navigator and cosmopolitan of the fifteenth century', as well as 'that economic realism which from an early date tended to correct the excesses of the military and religious spirit in the formation of Brazilian society' (pp. 9–10). Later on, he attributed several of the outstanding qualities of traveller and writer Fernão Mendes Pinto (c. 1509–1583) to the probable Jewish background of the author of the *Peregrinação* (1614) — a book that, Freyre held, epitomized the Portuguese spirit of the age of the geographical expansions.[23] Therefore, with their purportedly 'good' and 'bad' qualities, Freyre viewed Jews as essential elements of both 'Luso-tropicalism' and Brazilian nationhood. Also telling is Freyre's positive stance towards his Jewish contemporaries, such as his admiration for Boas and for certain Jewish intellectuals he met in New York. We should also bear in mind that *Casa-Grande & Senzala* was a rebuttal of the book *Raça e Assimilação* (1932), in which the jurist and sociologist Francisco José de Oliveira Viana (1886–1951) called for restrictions on racial miscegenation and immigration so as to neutralize, among other 'threats', the 'Semitic danger'.[24] Three years after *Casa-Grande & Senzala*, upon publication of *Sobrados e Mucambos*, Freyre accepted the invitation of Uri Zwerling (1893–1967) to participate with other renowned intellectuals in the book *Os Judeus na História do Brasil* (1936). According to Nachman Falbel, this collection of short historical pieces sought to demonstrate 'the extent to which Jews, since Cabral's discovery, are profoundly linked to the formation of the country since its beginning and their unique contribution, starting with the New Christians,

---

[21] Chiavenato, *O inimigo eleito*, p. 272. An identical claim is argued by Cortez Silva, *Tempos de Casa-Grande (1930–1940)*, p. 226.
[22] Cortez Silva, 'O discurso anti-Semita na obra de Gilberto Freyre', p. 347.
[23] Gilberto Freyre, 'Fernão Mendes Pinto, tropicalista', in idem, *O Luso e o Trópico*, cap. VII, pp. 141 ss.
[24] Jeffrey Lesser, *Welcoming the Undesirables: Brazil and the Jewish Question* (Berkeley: University of California Press, 1995), esp. pp. 33, 54, 67, 84, 109; idem, 'Metáforas de uma civilização', in *O anti-Semitismo nas Américas*, ed. by Tucci Carneiro, pp. 317–21.

which were decisive for the social and economic development, from the early sixteenth century to our times, being active participants in all the stages of Brazil's economic history'.[25] Thus, Freyre contributed to debunking the notion of Jews as eternal foreigners, a popular anti-Semitic trope of the time.[26]

In the preface to the second English edition of *Casa-Grande & Senzala* (1956), Freyre admitted that, initially, 'some Jewish leaders' had accused him of anti-Semitism. Now, though, he claimed, '[s]ome outstanding Jewish leaders in Europe, the United States, and Latin America have publicly acknowledged my work as an endeavor to do justice to the Jewish contribution to Iberian civilization' (p. xix). In the preface to the sixth Portuguese edition (1950), Freyre had already mentioned the writer and activist Camille Honig (1905–1977) as one of those Jewish leaders that had praised his book.[27] Freyre's ideas on hybridity and miscegenation do, indeed, seem to have served as inspiration for Honig, in his claim that Jews are not a race.[28] Furthermore, in the view of Peter Burke and Maria Pallares Burke, one can detect Freyre's influence in 'Brazil, Country of the Future' (1941) by Stefan Zweig (1881–1942), Honig's friend and mentor, who maintained that Brazil, the country where he had found refuge, was far from the national and racial exclusivities that marked the Old Continent.[29] In 1955, Freyre wrote a preface to the essay 'O anti-semitismo no Brasil: tentativa de interpretação sociológica' by his young fellow countryman, the sociologist Vamireh Chacon. Even if Freyre preferred not to take a stance against anti-Semitism and instead complimented Chacon's approach to what he called 'a delicate and complex' question, it is a fact that his introduction, along with Chacon's text, was published by the Jewish 'Hebraica Club' of Recife.[30] Indeed, today, there are those who choose to minimize expressions of prejudice in Freyre's works and describe him as a pioneer recognizing the positive role of the 'Semitic element' in Brazil, especially in his native Northeastern region.[31] To summarize: we can affirm, as Jeffrey Lesser did, that '[e]ven Gilberto Freyre,

---

[25] Nachman Falbel, 'Uri Zwerling e a literatura antissemita no Brasil', in Uri Zwerling, *Os judeus na história do Brasil*, ed. by Any Dana (Rio de Janeiro: Outras Letras Editora, 2013), pp. 11–28 (p. 20).
[26] Gilberto Freyre, 'Os começos da literatura israelita na América', in *Os judeus no história do Brasil*, ed. by Zwerling, pp. 117–19.
[27] Idem, *Casa-Grande & Senzala*, op. cit., p. 85.
[28] E.g. Camille Honig, 'Is there a Jewish Race?', *The California Jewish Voice*, 25 September 1953.
[29] It is a fragile supposition, actually, considering what Alberto Dines related when presenting a late testimony by Freyre himself, denying this possibility because of a conversation with the Austrian essayist in which Zweig never mentioned having read Freyre's book (Alberto Dines, *Morte no paraíso: a tragédia de Stefan Zweig* (Rio de Janeiro: Nova Fronteira, 1981), p. 248).
[30] Vamireh Chacon, *O antis-semitismo no Brasil: tentativa de interpretação sociológica* (Recife: Clube Hebraico, 1955), pp. 5–6 (= Gilberto Freyre, *Prefácios Desgarrados*. Organização do texto introdução e notas de Edson Nery da Fonseca, 2 vols (Rio de Janeiro: Cátedra, 1978), I, 508–09).
[31] Marcos Chor Maio, '"Estoque Semita": a presença dos Judeus em *Casa-grande & Senzala*', *Luso-Brazilian Review*, 36.1 (1999), 95–110; idem, 'Os judeus no pensamento de Gilberto Freyre', in *Seminário Internacional Novo Mundo nos Trópicos*, ed. by Fátima Quintas (Recife: Fundação Gilberto Freyre, 2000), pp. 67–70; Cesar Sobreira, *Nordeste Semita: ensaio sobre um certo Nordeste que em Gilberto Freyre também é semita* (São Paulo: Global, 2009); idem, 'Gilberto Freyre e o Judaísmo: reflexões sobre o Pathos semítico no Judeu de Apipucos',*Ciência & Trópico, Recife*, 34 (2010), 325–42.

who openly defended Jews as one component of Brazilian "racial democracy", was deeply influenced by the negative stereotypes'.[32]

3

How might we approach the conflict between those who identify an 'anti-Semitic discourse' in *Casa-Grande & Senzala* and those who advance a 'philo-Semitic' articulation of it? According to Jeffrey D. Needell, this discrepancy results from Freyre's ambivalence about modernity, which he symbolically associated with Jews.[33] A cosmopolitan intellectual of the urban classes, Freyre was part of the alienating, crushing modernity he himself criticized.[34] This modernity characterized his very own country, the urbanized and industrialized Brazil of the twentieth century. The modernizing figure of the 'Jew' appears in Freyre's books as an impetus of historical dynamism, acting against the conservative weight of the traditions of other peoples and cultures — be it in medieval Portugal or in colonial Brazil — through a generalized process of interaction between opposing poles, which Freyre called a 'balance between antagonisms'.[35] In his 'Brazil: An Interpretation' (1947), a synthetic work published originally in English, Freyre provided an example of what he meant by 'balance between antagonisms' in the case of the 'Jews'. While he acknowledged the evil generated by the 'Jews' in Brazil with the creation of a slave economy, the vigorous sugar industry was an engine of positive progress.[36]

Needell rightly detected in Freyre's works a metaphysical, troubled view of the Jew and Judaism (what he conceived as their 'flaws' and 'virtues') that ultimately produces positivity because it constitutes a dialectical polarity in the historical making. We ought to remember, however, that shortly afterwards Freyre affirms that '[f]ortunately for both Portugal and Brazil' this modernization put an end to the 'traditional love' that 'the so-called *portugueses velhos*' had for the land, 'who would be the basic human element of the agrarian colonization of Brazil'.[37] Those Freyre called 'portugueses velhos' were peasants from Portugal's heartland who did not mingle with Jews or New Christians and consequently preserved their pristine character. These farmers, Freyre

---

[32] Lesser, *Welcoming the Undesirables*, p. 35.
[33] Jeffrey D. Needell, 'Identity, Race, Gender, and Modernity in the Origins of Gilberto Freyre's Oeuvre', *The American Historical Review*, 100 (1995), 51–77.
[34] Idem, p. 75.
[35] 'From a general point of view, the formation of Brazilian society, as I stressed from the first pages of this essay, has been in reality, a process of balancing antagonisms...' (Freyre, *The Masters and the Slaves [Casa-Grande & Senzala]. A Study in the Development of Brazilian Civilization*, pp. 79–80).
[36] 'This antagonism, however, must be regarded by the students of early Brazilian history not only as an evil — for it was an evil — but also as a stimulus of differentiation and progress [...] [b]ut this antagonism was, in more than one respect, beneficial to Portuguese America. Urban Jews with a genius for trade made possible the industrialization of sugar-cane agriculture in Brazil and the successful commercialization of Brazilian sugar'. I consulted the second edition, which came with a different title: Gilberto Freyre, *Brazil: An Interpretation* (New York: Alfred A. Knopf, 1947), pp. 13–14.
[37] Idem, pp. 12–13.

concludes, *ipso facto* were at the mercy of the others who, with the tricks and greedy speculations of the Jews, exploited the tropics. Bearing this in mind, one ought to notice that Freyre maintains the hybrid character of the Portuguese and the Brazilians and, at the same time, identifies the existence of groups that are immune to the 'Semitic influence'. Moreover, when Freyre refers to the beginning of Brazilian colonization in Brazil in *Casa-Grande & Senzala*, he describes a heterogeneous group of immigrants, among whom were conversos (e.g., p. 30). In another passage, Freyre asserts the likelihood of there having been, among the first settlers, various people of Muslim origins, together with the New Christians and Old Portuguese (p. 219). How are we to understand the apparent contradiction between a narrative of hybrid miscegenation and the recognition of the permanence of ethnically differentiated groups?

4

To address this question, I will delve into a topic of wide-ranging debate among scholars of Freyre: the affinity or lack thereof in *Casa-Grande & Senzala* with the thought of Franz Boas concerning the relationship between race and culture (pp. xxvi–xxxii). We know that Boas denied the existence of fixed racial characteristics because of the structuring influence of culture and natural environment. In the case of the Jews, Boas went so far as to question the accuracy of conceiving them as a race in the face of extreme geographical dispersion and its modifying effects to the physiognomy and personality of their members.[38] In contrast, *Casa-Grande & Senzala* presents a well-defined 'Jewish being'. Following Ricardo Benzaquén de Araújo, Marcos Chor Maio argues that Freyre adopts positions that are more properly defined as neo-Lamarckian than Boasian.[39] This seems valid in the case of Africans transplanted to Brazil as slaves, as Freyre describes characteristics acquired during captivity and cultivated over generations (e.g., pp. 329–30). However, when Freyre deals with Jews and conversos, it is as if they carry characteristics that resist cultural and environmental change. On the one hand, for instance, Freyre explains the disdain of many Portuguese for farm labour as stemming from a 'Semitic' influence (here used as a synonym for Judaism), assuming the first settlers in Brazil would have preferred to find the economic situation the Portuguese had in India, 'in the manner of the Israelites [*israelitamente*], carry on trade in spices and precious stones', instead of confronting a land with uncertain farming potential. On the other hand, this initial disappointment forced these settlers to adapt that commercial disposition to the Brazilian situation,

---

[38] Thus, for example, when describing '[t]he modifications, possibly due to environment, to be found in the descendants of immigrants — as in the case of the Sicilian and German Jews studied by Boas in the United States [...]' (Freyre, *The Masters and the Slaves [Casa-Grande & Senzala]. A Study in the Development of Brazilian Civilization*, p. xxxi).

[39] Benzaquén de Araújo, *Guerra e Paz*, pp. 27–41; Chor Maio, '"Estoque Semita"', *passim*.

resulting first in the exploitation of Brazil wood and then in the sugar industry (p. 33). From this example, we can infer that the inclination of the 'Jews' for commerce was the best means to survive environmental shifts, in a way that left their constitutional characteristics intact. Commercial versatility, then, was not the result of acculturation or accommodation. On the contrary: commercial versatility was the very secret of 'Jewish' endurance across time and space.

Chor Maio also argues that Freyre's conception of the 'Jew' was related to ideas of Max Weber. Although Freyre adduces the authority of Weber in *Casa-Grande & Senzala*, the book does not depict the alleged Jewish proclivity for commercial activities as the result of certain social and historical specific conditions. Freyre cites Weber to depict a transformation of the Jews into 'technicians of usury' that involved 'an almost biological process of specialization', without indicating a neatly circumscribed historical period, but attributed to a loose 'ritualistic determinism, which after their exile forbade their settling in any land and becoming tillers of the soil' (p. 230). This reveals that for him, under circumstantial and evolutionary appearances, the proper economic and physical characteristics of the 'semitic' Jews and New Christians were generated in an indeterminate old mythical *illo tempore*. In this reification of the 'Jew', racial mixture seems to be the only medium by which one can modify the intensity of those characteristics by diluting them within the rest of society. Never, however, is the essence of the 'Jewish' tendencies touched upon.

Remarkably, in *Casa-Grande & Senzala*, the terms 'Jew' and 'New Christian' figure interchangeably. Let us recall that Portugal's Jews were forcibly baptized *en masse* by order of King Manuel I, in 1497, creating a pervasive converso or New Christian phenomenon. Although New Christians were not religiously homogeneous, they were suspected of being attached to the religion of their ancestors and were persecuted by the Inquisition. Here, though, Freyre was not alone: whether hostile or sympathetic, many Iberian scholars of the time often endorsed such a simplistic identification. That said, Freyre did not consider religious conversion an important factor in physical or behavioural change, because he perceived Judaism as a dominant essence. Thus, there are two forms of articulating the 'Jew' in Freyre's system of 'balance of antagonisms'. On the one hand, they appear as an ethnically differentiated group (e.g., the New Christians) that interacts with others (e.g., the 'Old Portuguese') through 'antagonisms' or clashes of idiosyncrasies (e.g., economic exploitation). On the other hand, there are identifiable 'Semitic' remains in Portuguese and Brazilian societies, and their 'balancing' is a harmonization that results from past miscegenation. Among them, signs such as '[t]he very ring on the finger of the Brazilian bachelor of arts or one holding a doctor's degree, a ring set with an emerald or ruby, impresses us as being reminiscent of the Orient and the Israelites', 'the mania for eyeglasses and pince-nez — employed as an outward mark of learning or of intellectual and scientific attainment', and the speculation that the recurrent use of the term *doutor* in Brazil by 'our bookkeepers who are bachelors of commerce, our agronomists, our engineers, our veterinarians — what is all this if not another Sephardic reminiscence?' (p. 233). Hence, one can infer that the more miscegenation, the more changes there are in these harmonizations or balancing effects. As we have seen, this was precisely what Freyre identifies as the true essence of the history of Portugal and Brazil. More than a fusion of neo-Lamarckism and Weber, then, the view of Jews and conversos found in Freyre's book coincides with the view of the defenders of the 'Laws of purity of blood' in the Iberian Peninsula during the early modern period, with all the contradictions, imprecisions, negotiations and fluctuations that characterized that proto-racial discourse.[40] Nevertheless, while the old defenders of the segregation of Jewish converts to Christianity and of their New Christian offspring thought of miscegenation as a deleterious contamination of Iberian society and Catholic religion, the author of *Casa-Grande & Senzala* perceives it as constitutive of Portuguese and Brazilian culture and identity. At this point, we shall turn from Freyre's anthropological views on history to an analysis of his stance on the historiographical views of his greatest guide in this domain: João Lúcio de Azevedo.

5

In the preface to the first edition of *Casa-Grande & Senzala*, Freyre relates that during his stay in Portugal between 1930 and 1931 he visited Azevedo several times while preparing the manuscript of his book. Of all Portuguese intellectuals, Azevedo was the only one who merited the epithet 'admirable scholar' (p. xxiv) and his influence is notable throughout the book. Biographical and historiographical ties brought Azevedo close to Brazil and to Freyre. At age eighteen, Azevedo left his native Portugal and moved to Brazil, first working as a salesman in the bookstore 'Livraria Tavares Cardoso' in the city of Belém and then becoming its owner. During nearly three decades in the northern Brazilian state of Pará, Azevedo conducted his first historical enquiries and obtained Brazilian citizenship. After he returned to Europe, he wrote regularly to intellectuals and historians in Brazil, and the history of these two countries became a constant presence in his historiographic production.[41] There was also a certain ideological affinity between Azevedo and Freyre since both were part of the same conservative intellectual circle around the essayist Fidelino de Figueiredo (1888–1967), from Lisbon.[42]

Azevedo's *História dos Cristãos-Novos Portugueses* (1921) had a major impact

---

[40] On the relationship between the 'laws of purity of blood' and racism, see Francisco Bethencourt, *Racisms: From Crusades to the Twentieth Century* (Princeton, NJ, and Oxford: Princeton University Press, 2013), pp. 148–51.
[41] Ana Luiza Marques Bastos, 'O historiador luso-brasileiro João Lúcio de Azevedo (1855–1933)', in *De colonos a imigrantes: i(e)migração portuguesa para o Brasil*, ed. by José Jobson de Andrade Arruda, Vera Lucia Amaral Ferlini, Maria Izilda Santos de Matos and Fernando de Sousa (São Paulo: Alameda, 2013), pp. 271–76.
[42] Larreta & Giucci, *Gilberto Freyre*, pp. 208–09.

on Freyre's historical view of Jews and conversos. From that book, Freyre learned of the centrality and permanence of the Jewish minority in Portugal, as well as the fact that this was one of the most prominent features of its history. Just as Freyre did later on, Azevedo made use of racist terms laced with anti-Semitic stereotypes, while asserting the intellectual superiority of Jews as well as their remarkable capacity for adaptation.[43] Like Freyre, Azevedo saw no substantial change resulting from the 'chimerical' forced baptism of Portugal's Jews in 1497 and their transformation into New Christians.[44] Freyre would agree with Azevedo in maintaining that the 'Jewish Question' was particularly manifest in the economic area, 'created by the irritating presence of a powerful suction-mechanism operating upon the majority of the people' (p. 230).[45] The historical comparison drawn by Azevedo in his *Novas epanáforas* (1932) between what happened in Portugal, where conversos were accused of 'refusing to work the land', and in colonial Brazil, where they had become farmers because 'beyond the Atlantic, agriculture was a form of industrial exploitation', was echoed by Freyre in *Casa-Grande & Senzala*, albeit in *more anthropologico*.[46]

Nevertheless, Freyre and Azevedo diverged on the issue of 'antagonisms'. According to Azevedo, the history of Jews and New Christians was a succession of clashes, because 'the antagonism in ethnic origins and conception of the divine' with the 'strange race' was an 'important factor of social imbalance'.[47] The Jews, Azevedo recalls, had long ago arrived in Portugal driven 'by the nomad instinct and the love of profit',[48] being strangers '[to] the nationality, whose features came from the Latin and Gothic elements'.[49] The title of the second chapter of his *História dos Cristãos-Novos Portugueses* broadcasts this view: 'Jews in Portugal: Antagonism between Races'. It is not surprising, then, that Azevedo sees the establishment of the Inquisition in 1536, or the strengthening of the anti-converso 'Laws of purity of blood' in Portugal, as organic reactions by the Old Christian majority to the unassimilable character of the Jewish-New Christian minority. Azevedo added that, compared to the violent *pogroms* that took place in other parts of Europe in past and present times, those were relatively moderate means of channelling an understandable 'social outrage'.[50] Nevertheless, those 'measures of social protection' could not stop the penetration of the 'Semitic influence' in Portugal. For Azevedo, the

---

[43] Azevedo, *História dos Cristãos-Novos Portugueses*, pp. 3-4, 15, 35-37.
[44] '[...] and the New Christian kept being the same hoarder of wealth, the same cruel usurer, the same speculator of public misery [...] for which the Iberian monarchs' assumption that the baptism was going to solve the "Jewish Question" was a chimera' (idem, pp. 39, 53-54).
[45] Idem, p. 34.
[46] João Lúcio de Azevedo, *Novas epanáforas: estudos de história e literatura* (Lisbon: Livraria Clássica de A. M. Teixeira, 1932), p. 140.
[47] Azevedo, *História dos Cristãos-Novos Portugueses*, pp. ix, 1.
[48] Idem, p. 2.
[49] Idem, 'Estudos para a história dos cristãos novos em Portugal', *Revista de História*, 2 (1912), 65-73 (p. 67).
[50] Idem, *História dos Cristãos-Novos Portugueses*, p. 48.

emergence of patently Jewish-inflected Portuguese Messianic *Sebastianismo* and the active participation of conversos in colonial commerce proved the pervasiveness of Jewish influence.[51]

Freyre, for his part, cherished the 'antagonisms' Azevedo deplored; after all, they yielded, as we have seen, fruitful 'balances'. Inspired by the liberal historian Alexandre Herculano (1810–1877), he averred that Portugal's own national origins ('the base and sinews of Portuguese nationality') derived from a mixture of Moorish and Christian blood during the Muslim conquest of the Iberian Peninsula and the Christian *Reconquista* wars (p. 209), and added that '[w]hat happened in the case of the Moors happened also, to a certain extent, with the Jews' (p. 216).[52] It is true that, both for Herculano and Freyre, Jews as a group, 'being somewhat strange to their milieu', had abused the tolerance granted by the majority with the improper use of their 'mercantile genius'. Hence, the establishment of the Inquisition was created, according to Freyre, 'less by reason of their religion, looked upon as an abomination, than by what was regarded as an utter lack of delicacy of feeling in their dealings with Christians where money matters were concerned' (p. 207). Notwithstanding this, Freyre asserted that, during the Middle Ages, Jews allied with the Christian nobility and the religious orders. Together, they exploited the common people. This alliance of economic interests eventually generated a process of miscegenation between the Christian and the Jewish elites: '[t]he blood of the best of Portugal's nobility thus mingled with that of the Hebraic plutocracy when fidalgos threatened with ruin took to wife the daughters of rich stockjobbers' (pp. 230–31). That explains, together with the influence of Moors and black slaves, the transformation of Portugal from 'an ancient people of husbandmen-kings into the most commercial and least rural of any in Europe' (p. 32). Thus, Freyre inferred that 'Portuguese imperialism and imperialist expansion were based upon Jewish prosperity' (p. 232), including the colonization of Brazil. Nothing the author of *Casa-Grande & Senzala* wrote could be further from what his mentor wrote in *História dos Cristãos-Novos Portugueses*.

It comes as little surprise, then, that although he bore anti-Semitic biases, Freyre opposed Mário Saa (1893–1971), a conservative author who wished to inject into the Portuguese world that racial anti-Semitic hatred that was spreading throughout Europe at the time (p. 229). For Freyre, the racialist criteria Saa supported in his rant *A invasão dos Judeus* (1925) was both patently absurd and needlessly harmful. There was no sense, he wrote, in distinguishing

---

[51] Ibid, p. 46. In a study that Azevedo published on the subject in 1916 he claimed: 'Sebastianism came from the Jewish hope for the Messiah, mixed with the late prophecies brought from Spain, and remnants of legends from the Arthurian cycle, preserved in folk tradition' (idem, *A evolução do Sebastianismo* (Lisbon: Editorial Presença, 1984), pp. 8–9).

[52] Although Herculano condemned the Inquisition for being an obscurantist institution contrary to the spirit of the Gospels, he did not hesitate in describing Jews in Portugal as ungrateful for the protection and tolerance of Portuguese institutions. Cf. Alexandre Herculano, *History of the Origin and Establishment of the Inquisition in Portugal*, trans. by John C. Branner, Prolegomenon by Yosef Hayim Yerushalmi (New York: Ktav Publishing House Inc., 1972), pp. 239–49.

today between those who Saa identified as descending from New Christians and those who believed they came from Old Christians based on their physical traits and political leanings.[53] We must not forget that, for Freyre, the concept of Brazil as a 'racial democracy' or his idea that in Portugal it was 'impossible to draw conclusions from ethno-social stratifications in a people that has been so restless and so plastic in its movements' (p. 210) were facts to be reckoned with and not social-political projects to be realized. While it is true there is a recognizable '(philo-) Semitic stock' in *Casa-Grande & Senzala*, as Chor Maio notes, it is only manifested as a by-product of miscegenation. For Freyre, nevertheless, the 'Semitic stock' was ambivalent, because it included that notion of 'Israelite infiltration' defended by Azevedo (p. 9 n. 18). Hence, eliding, downplaying or sugar-coating anti-Semitic assumptions so as to savour felicitous 'philo-Semitic miscegenation' risks not only missing the complexity of Freyre's book but also ignoring the paradoxical mechanism Freyre used to build his influential narrative of *métissage* of Portuguese and Brazilian identity. I will discuss the implications of this through a comparison of *Casa-Grande & Senzala* and the work of one of Freyre's contemporaries, Américo Castro (1885–1972), whose view of Spain as a nationality also contemplates the contribution of Jews and conversos.

6

Freyre and Castro are close in biographical, historiographical and methodological terms. Castro was born in Brazil to Spanish parents. Although he returned with his family to Granada when he was four, his Brazilian origins facilitated his immigration to the United States after a period of uncertainty in Latin America (e.g., in Buenos Aires) as an exile from the Spanish Civil War. In 1940, he received a chair in Spanish at Princeton University, but by 1925 he had already acquired international prestige as a Hispanist with the publication of *El pensamiento de Cervantes*.[54] Thanks to the research of Alberto Dines, we know that Freyre unsuccessfully attempted to obtain an immigration visa for Castro to Brazil to contribute to the cultural and scientific advancement of the country.[55] Being an anti-Franco political dissenter, Castro shared neither the ideology of Vargas's regime nor Freyre's conservatism. But Castro was a prominent member of the Spanish 'Generation of '98', intellectuals who sought to redefine 'Spanishness' after the final collapse of the Spanish empire in 1898 by rediscovering its Iberian dimensions, through divergent interpretations.

[53] Cf. Mário Saa, *Portugal Cristão-Novo ou os Judeus na República* (Lisbon: Henrique Torres, 1921); idem, *A invasão dos Judeus* (Lisbon: Libânio da Silva, 1925).
[54] José Luis Gómez-Martínez, *Américo Castro y el origen de los españoles: historia de una polémica* (Madrid: Editorial Gredos, 1975); Edmund L. King, 'Introduction', in *Américo Castro: The Impact of his Thought: Essays to Mark the Centenary of his Birth*, ed. by Ronald E. Surtz, Jaime Ferrán and Daniel Testa (Madison, WI: The Hispanic Seminary of Medieval Studies, 1998), pp. ix–xv.
[55] Dines, *Morte no paraíso*, op. cit., pp. 224–25.

Thus, in the *Idearium español* (1897), the writer and diplomat Ángel Ganivet (1865–1898) repudiated entrenched Eurocentric views of the Iberian Peninsula by recognizing the Arab contribution.

Freyre was introduced to pan-Iberian thought during his stay in Lisbon in 1923, when he visited the conservative ideologue of Portuguese 'Integralismo Lusitano' and anti-Semitic writer António Sardinha (1888–1925).[56] Through Sardinha, Freyre found one of the independent, conservative Spanish followers of 'the Generation of '98', Ramiro de Maeztu (1875–1936), who claimed in his *La defensa de la hispanidad* (1934) that 'the Spanish character was formed in a centuries'-long struggle between Moors and Jews'.[57] Nevertheless, in *Casa-Grande & Senzala*, Freyre adopted a Ganivet-like pan-Iberianism, as stemming from a 'close resemblance in character' between Portugal and Castile which paradoxically produced an 'historic anthypathy' (p. 249). At the same time, Freyre explained that the Portuguese were even 'more cosmopolitan' than the Spanish, for the Portuguese 'is probably the less Gothic, and the more Semitic, the less European and the more African of the two' (p. 8 n. 16). This attitude can be traced to his abandonment of prejudices against miscegenation in the course of his work with Boas (p. 32).

Castro's name does not feature in *Casa-Grande & Senzala* or even in *Sobrados e Mucambos*. Only after the most suggestive works by Castro such as *España en su historia* (1948), *Aspectos del vivir hispánico* (1947) and, especially, *La realidad histórica de España* (1954, which is an expanded re-edition of *España en su historia*) had been published, do we find the Princeton scholar cited by the author of *Casa-Grande & Senzala*.[58] Like Freyre, Castro rejects Eurocentric perspectives to argue that Spain did not originate with Romans and Goths alone. In his view, Spain was produced from a phenomenon of '*convivencia*' — living together — generated after the Muslim invasion in the eighth century and consolidated during the reign of Alfonso X 'El Sabio' (1221–1284), a Christian monarch who integrated the contributions of Muslims and Jews and thus endorsed a clear consciousness of 'Spanishness'. Since the fifteenth century on, this three-dimensional, synergetic *convivencia* reached its highest political, religious and cultural level with the integration of 'Hispano-Hebrew' values by

---

[56] Gilberto Freyre, 'António Sardinha', *Revista do Norte* (Recife), 1 (1925), 5–6; idem, *Tempo de aprendiz: artigos publicados em jornais na adolescência e primeira mocidade do autor, 1918–1926* (São Paulo and Brasília: IBRASA- INL, 1979), pp. 277–78.

[57] Gómez-Martínez, *Américo Castro y el origen de los españoles*, pp. 13–33.

[58] Both books are connected. On the one hand, *España en su historia* was ready in 1946 but was published two years later, for reasons 'beyond its author's control' (Américo Castro, *España en su historia: cristianos, moros y judíos* (Barcelona: Crítica, 1983), p. 17). 'Aspectos del vivir hispánico' was written by Castro right afterwards, although the initial idea came from a series of essays written in 1939 under the title 'Lo hispánico y el erasmismo', which had appeared in *Revista de filología hispánica* in 1941–1942 (Américo Castro, *Aspectos del vivir hispánico: espiritualismo, mesianismo, actitud personal en los siglos XIV al XVI* (Santiago de Chile: Editorial Cruz del Sur, 1947), pp. 9–10). 'La realidad histórica de España' was an expansion of these two books. I use the following edition: Américo Castro, *La realidad histórica de España, edición renovada* (Mexico: Editorial Porrua, 1962).

the Iberian society, thanks to the mediation of the conversos.⁵⁹ Castro's ideas were part of lively debates between renowned Spanish intellectuals such as the philosopher José Ortega y Gasset (1883–1955), for whom Spain was an offshoot of its Visigoth past, and particularly, the historian Claudio Sánchez Albornoz (1893–1984), for whom, contrary to Castro, 'the Spaniard' was the by-product of a longstanding struggle against the Muslims and the Jews. Years later, the philologist Eugenio Asensio (1902–1996) criticized what he thought was Castro's arbitrary overestimation of the contribution of the conversos to Spanish Catholicism, literature and the arts during the 'The Golden Age'.⁶⁰ Nevertheless, Castro's ideas animated those who had celebrated racial miscegenation and the 'balance of antagonisms' as constitutive values of Portuguese and Brazilian national identities. Freyre left a testimony to this identification in the notes he penned in his copy of *La realidad histórica de España*: one can read in its page margins '*Casa-Grande & Senzala*'.⁶¹ In addition, from the 1950s on, Freyre quoted Castro's work to develop his own ideas, even expanding his concept of 'Luso-tropicalism' to 'Iberian-tropicalism' to reflect his notion of a common Iberian manner of perceiving time, originating from distant Arab-Muslim substrata.⁶²

As for the Jews and conversos, we recall that, unlike Castro, Freyre did not make them the main protagonists of *Casa-Grande & Senzala* — they only appear as antagonists or remnants of the past. However, I believe that when, in the preface to the second English edition, Freyre claimed that the initial accusations of anti-Semitism became expressions of gratitude for valuing the contribution of Jews to the Iberian civilization, he was invoking Castro's arguments to defend himself against a charge that had become acutely infamous after the Nazi horrors.⁶³ Castro, however, understood 'Spanishness' very differently to the way Freyre defined 'Brazilianness'. It is true that both scholars relied on Oswald Spengler (1880–1936) and his idea that every culture was a totalizing living and interacting organism. But while Freyre emphasized the influence of environment on race ('Spengler stresses the point that a race does not migrate from one continent to another; for that it would be necessary to transport along

---

⁵⁹ A summary of Castro's positions is found in the preface to the new edition of *La realidad histórica de España* (idem, pp. xi–xxviii).

⁶⁰ Gómez-Martínez, *Américo Castro y el origen de los españoles*, pp. 34–59; idem, 'Américo Castro y Sánchez-Albornoz: dos posiciones ante el origen de los españoles', *Nueva Revista de filología hispánica*, 21.2 (1972), 301–20; Eugenio Asensio, *La España imaginada de Américo Castro. Edición corregida y aumentada* (Barcelona: Editorial Crítica, 1992); Albert Sicroff, 'Américo Castro and his Critics: Eugenio Asensio', *Hispanic Review*, 40.1 (1972), 1–30.

⁶¹ Peter Burke and Maria Lúcia G. Pallares-Burke, *Gilberto Freyre: Social Theory in the Tropics* (Oxford: Lang, 2008), pp. 97, 226, n. 135.

⁶² Gilberto Freyre, 'A propósito de hispanos', in *Seleta para jovens. Organizada pelo autor com a colaboração de Maria Elisa Dias Collier* (Rio de Janeiro: Livraria José Olympo Editora, 1971), pp. 80–83. Cf. Alberto Luiz Schneider, 'Iberismo e luso-tropicalismo na obra de Gilberto Freyre', *Revista de História da Historiografia* (Ouro Preto), 10 (2012), 75–93.

⁶³ Freyre, *The Masters and the Slaves [Casa-Grande & Senzala]. A Study in the Development of Brazilian Civilization*, p. xix.

with it the physical environment', p. xxxi), Castro relied on Spengler's concept of *'pseudo-morphose'* to argue that in Spain there were cultural, superimposed, mutually influencing and erupting strata. Those differences in perspective follow from the fact that Freyre's sociological and anthropological approaches do not correspond to Castro's culturalism, derived from the *Weltanschauungen* ideas of the philosopher Wilhelm Dilthey (1833–1911). Hence, while, for Freyre, it is through the analysis of everyday life (work, sexual relations, gastronomy) that one grasps the workings of a society, for Castro, literary production best expresses the values of the group as bearer of specific experience (*Erlebnis*) and self-consciousness of something experienced (*Selbstbesinnung*).[64] Thus, Castro referred to Christians, Moors and Jews as 'castes' bearing idiosyncratic characteristics or psychological traits rather than 'races', as did Freyre, 'because these indicate something which is already fixed, motionless'.[65] According to Castro, the 'caste' was a prism of ethnic, social and cultural expression through which each group dynamically articulates its own 'living experience' and deals with others. The result of the prolonged interactions of the living experiences between Christian, Muslim and Jewish 'castes' was the historical specificity of Spain, departing from a relatively harmonious *convivencia* between those castes during the Middle Ages, through an unified synthesis created by a crisis during the 'conflictive era' of the sixteenth and seventeenth centuries, after the mass and often forced conversions to Christianity of Jews and Muslims.[66]

Castro's 'conflictive era' features a dialectical interaction between the Old and New Christians that is highly reminiscent of Freyre's 'balance of antagonisms'. Nevertheless, rather than discussing 'miscegenation', Castro favours the term 'symbiosis' to depict the cultural interaction between 'castes'. Perhaps one might apply the term 'hybridization' to both authors, since this fashionable concept has become a convenient way of referring to all cultural exchange and human interaction, without necessarily specifying the historical conditions and the price of obtaining these colourful by-products.[67] Furthermore, I have detected an analogous mechanism in Freyre's and Castro's narratives to conjoin the contribution of Jews and conversos to the national narratives. It is true that in *Casa-Grande & Senzala*, Jewish 'flaws' and 'virtues' are related in an impersonal manner while in Castro's works they are introduced via myriad authors, literary works and specific ideologies. However, when Castro wished to show the 'Hispano-Hebrew' influence, he often presumed what was thought to be truly 'Jewish'. According to Asensio, these presumptions prevailed in the conversos' case because 'what [Castro] defines as Jewish [*hebreo*] may be simply

---

[64] Castro, *La realidad histórica de España*, p. 141 n. 4. Cf. Asensio, *La España imaginada de Américo Castro*, p. 40; Francisco Márquez Villanueva, 'Américo Castro y la historia', in *Américo Castro: The Impact of his Thought*, ed. by Surtz, Ferrán and Testa, pp. 127–39 (p. 134).
[65] Castro, *La realidad histórica de España*, p. 110.
[66] Ibid, pp. 54, 67; Américo Castro, *De la edad conflictiva* (Madrid: Taurus, 1961).
[67] Marwan M. Kraidy, *Hybridity: The Cultural Logic of Globalization* (Philadelphia, PA: Temple University Press, 2005).

subjective, universally human or commonly European, either Christian or Jewish'.[68] Thus, according to this critic, the chasm that seemed to set Castro's eminent sympathy towards the 'Jew' apart from Freyre's anti-Semitic prejudices is questioned by analogous assumptions. In other words, even if Castro declared that he rejected the static categories of identity such as 'race', opting for existential notions such as 'life experience' ('*vividura*') or 'disposition and way of life',[69] his recognition of 'Hispano-Hebrew' imprints reveals that 'only an obscure faith in the strength of blood could justify the constant slip from the mere stating of a race to attributing gestures and modes of sensibility that are supposedly typical of conversos'.[70] For Asensio, through these paradoxes, Castro identified in the Inquisition and the 'Laws of purity of blood' two of the many contributions of the 'Hispano-Hebrews' to the Spanish character. Assuming that there was a Jewish-Sephardic obsession with lineage and that public denunciations were common within medieval Jewish communities, Castro held that conversos transmitted those elements of their past Jewish particular existence into the broad society through their Christianization and institutional adaptation.[71] Those negative converso contributions to Spanishness were exceptional in Castro's otherwise sympathetic work, and perhaps because of that they were the only ones accepted by Sánchez Albornoz as well.[72] This explains how two eminent historians of Sephardi Judaism, namely, Yitzhak Baer (1888–1980) and Benzion Netanyahu (1910–2012), linked Castro with his fiercest critic.[73] Accordingly, Castro's and Sánchez Albornoz's mistakes stemmed from an ignorance of Hebrew sources and a slanted assessment of their historical contribution. According to Netanyahu, both relied on Ernest Renan (1823–1892) and his biased view of Jews and Judaism, a writer 'whose famous theory of human races contributed to the advent of modern anti-Semitism'.[74] Castro's

---

[68] Asensio, *La España imaginada de Américo Castro*, p. 44.
[69] Castro, *La realidad histórica de España*, p. 110.
[70] Asensio, *La España imaginada de Américo Castro*, p. 60.
[71] Castro, *España en su historia: cristianos, moros y judíos*, pp. 509–55. According to Miriam Bodian, Castro's views on medieval practising Jews were deeply negative (Miriam Bodian, 'Américo Castro's Conversos and the Question of Subjectivity', *Culture & History Digital Journal*, 6.2 <http://dx.doi.org/10.3989/chdj.2017.018>).
[72] 'Nowadays there is no doubt that the Inquisition was a Satanic Hispanic-Hebrew invention' (Claudio Sánchez Albornoz, *España, un enigma histórico*, 2 vols (Buenos Aires: Editorial Sudamericana, 1956), II, 255). Cf. idem, pp. 285–92. On Sánchez-Albornoz's anti-Semitic views, see Yosef Kaplan, 'Between Yitzhak Baer and Claudio Sánchez Albornoz: The Rift that Never Healed', in *Jewish Culture in Early Modern Europe: Essays in Honor of David B. Ruderman*, ed. by Richard I. Cohen, Natalie B. Dohrmann, Adam Shear and Elchanan Reiner (Pittsburgh, PA: University of Pittsburgh Press; Cincinnati, OH: Hebrew Union College Press, 2014), pp. 356–68.
[73] Benzion Netanyahu, 'Américo Castro and his View of the Origins of the Pureza de Sangre', *Proceedings of the American Academy for Jewish Research*, 46–47 (1978–79), 397–457; idem, 'Sánchez-Albornoz' View of Jewish History in Spain', in idem, *Toward the Inquisition: Essays on Jewish and Converso History in Late Medieval Spain* (Ithaca, NY, and London: Cornell University Press, 1997), pp. 126–55; Yitzhak Baer, *Historia de los judíos en la España cristiana*, 2 vols (Madrid: Altalena, 1981), II, 655–63.
[74] Netanyahu, 'Sánchez-Albornoz' View of Jewish History in Spain', pp. 132–33; idem, 'Américo Castro and his View of the Origins of the Pureza de Sangre', p. 399 n. 6.

followers, for their part, rejected the linkage of Castro, who had generally identified the best of the Spanish genius with the 'Hispano-Hebrew' influence, with Sánchez Albornoz, who claimed that 'the contribution of the Spanish Jews to the formation of the Hispanic was very different and always negative in character, in the sense that it did not transfer qualities but provoked reactions. Nothing essential in the psychic structure of the Jewish people left traces in the Spaniards. Besides, the Hebrew and the Hispanic are always in unquestionable opposition'.[75] *Mutatis mutandis*, Freyre as much as Castro was charged with melding bias and inclusion.

7

As mentioned *en passant*, Freyre's political views in his youth were more liberal and radical than afterwards. After holding an ambivalent position vis-à-vis the autocratic Vargas Era (1930–1945), in the 1950s and 1960s he overtly supported Portugal's Salazar regime, including its colonialist policies, and the military dictatorship in Brazil. Considering the fact that his anti-Jewish views were expressed only before the 1940s, Freyre's later political conservativism appears to have coincided with an identification with Castro's more positive views on Jews and Judaism. Hence, beyond considering Freyre's intellectual biography in order to understand how 'anti-Semitism' and 'philo-Semitism' converged in a single narrative, I suggest that *Casa-Grande & Senzala* shares a historiographic genre with Castro's works. Both Freyre and Castro exploited the notion of hybridization to refute the then-prevailing essentialist assumptions of nationalist and ethnocentric historiography. We see in both cases a paradox: in order to ascribe a hybrid character to the societies they studied from the perspective of encounters between different cultures and human groups, both authors had to articulate assumptions about 'the Jew'. For Freyre — unlike Castro — that essentialist vision was recurrent rather than occasional. This is because, like his mentor, Boas, Freyre did not conceive of the dispersed Jewish minority as a culture unto itself, like Afro-Americans or Native Americans.[76] Without granting to Judaism a civilizational dimension, or even a concept such as Castro's 'caste', Freyre insisted on those then-fashionable ideas about the Jewish mentality, their economic leanings or their physiognomy.[77] In an article published in 1923 in the *Diário de Pernambuco* about the growing presence of Jewish immigrants in the Northeast of Brazil, Freyre recognized that this was 'at the same time an advantage and *the shadow of a danger*'. In line with the critical outline Hannah Arendt (1906–1975) will later give us of the Jewish pro-emancipation discourse since the end of the

---

[75] Sánchez Albornoz, *España, un enigma histórico*, II, 164.
[76] Leonard B. Glick, 'Types Distinct from our Own: Franz Boas on Jewish Identity and Assimilation', *American Anthropologist*, New Series, 84 (1982), 545–65 (p. 561).
[77] Sander Gilman, *The Jew's Body* (New York and London: Routledge, 1991).

eighteenth century in *The Origins of Totalitarianism* (1951), Freyre claimed that, while Jewish 'exclusivism' could be a menace, there was no harm in finding Jews in the cities, for being an 'intelligent' and 'picturesque' element evoking the medieval 'ghettos'. Besides, Freyre claimed there were Jews who 'grow roots in the country of their nationality — tying blood to land'. According to Freyre, 'this kind of Jew could only be an advantage for a country in which the national "we"' dilutes their blood with no exclusivist preoccupations'. As an example, he pointed to Benjamin Disraeli (1804–1881), 'who was so identified with the English national destiny that he became for many years — already bearing the title of Lord Beaconsfield — the most authentic incarnation of the spirit of England and its most intimate traditions'.[78] Since *Casa-Grande & Senzala* was a portrait of colonial society, Freyre did not discuss there the potential for paternalistic tolerance and assimilation offered to Jews by the pro-emancipation model of nation-state analysed by Arendt. Thus, he described the way by which 'Jewish' idiosyncrasies were integrated into Luso-Brazilian societies though miscegenation, sowing the seeds of a pre-state hybrid nationhood. Consequently, I refrain from adopting the term 'allosemitism' promoted by Zygmunt Bauman as a concept that combines philo-Semitic and anti-Semitic elements in one discourse that conceives Jews as the 'radical other'.[79] On the one hand, for neither Freyre nor Castro is the Jew an alterity, since 'Portugalness', 'Brazilianness' and 'Spanishness' could not be conceived without its contribution. On the other hand, 'allosemitism' prevents us from identifying a specific way through which prejudice and integration, philo-Semitism and anti-Semitism, are articulated in one and the same discourse. Rather than arousing a sense of strangeness, philo-Semitic and anti-Semitic views often endorse mysterious and reified views of 'the Jew', thus enabling an easy handover from one view to the other. Thus, instead of revealing such a paradoxical construction of Jewishness, 'allosemitism' dilutes both polarities to create an amorphous and less politically loaded category.

In the present article, I have drawn a kind of archaeological sketch of the role of Jewishness in certain hybrid discourses of our time, which celebrate the contributions of those 'great Jews' who managed to abandon their 'parochial' and 'chauvinistic' particularism to make foundational contributions to humanity (e.g. Saint Paul, Baruch Spinoza, Karl Marx).[80] After the collapse of the nation-state, those who today celebrate miscegenated 'Jewish-Gentility' ('judéo-gentils' *dicit* Edgar Morin) as necessary hybridizations, for the good of a globalized world that aspires to be cleansed of xenophobic essentialism,

---

[78] Cortez Silva, *Tempos de Casa-Grande (1930–1940)*, p. 69. Cf. Hannah Arendt, *The Origins of Totalitarianism* (Orlando, FL: Harcourt Brace, 1976), pp. 56–57.

[79] Zygmunt Bauman, 'Allosemitism: Premodern, Modern, Postmodern', in *Modernity, Culture, and 'the Jew'*, ed. by Bryan Cheyette and Laura Marcus (Stanford, CA: Stanford University Press, 1998), pp. 143–56.

[80] Alain Badiou, *Circonstances 3: portées du mot 'juif'* (Paris: Leo Schéer, 2005); Edgar Morin, *Le Monde moderne et la question juive* (Paris: Le Seuil, 2006).

have shown sympathy for other alterities recognized as civilizations and justify their (provisional) survival in the name of a multicultural historical stage. I do not assign to Freyre responsibility for a problem with which many Jews are confronted today in certain alter-globalization hybrid discourses.[81] I only wish to emphasize a possible genealogical link between this problem and Freyre's *Casa-Grande & Senzala*. Peter Burke recently described the historiographical times in which we live in terms of an enthusiastic conversion to the narrative of hybridization: 'Some people whom may describe as "*purists*" were deeply shocked by the arguments of Freyre, Castro, and Toynbee when they were first published. Today, by contrast, many of us are prepared to find hybridizations almost everywhere in history. In an age of cultural globalization — even if the strength of this movement is sometimes exaggerated — historians are increasingly sensitized to similar phenomena in the past'.[82] Sharing Burke's satisfaction with the escape from the chimera of identity essentialism, in this article I have sought to call attention to one of the possible paradoxical outcomes of the 'mestizo mind'. It was not by chance that Burke mentioned Arnold Toynbee (1889-1975) as a pioneer of hybrid historiography, alongside Freyre and Castro. When Toynbee celebrated human diversity and challenged national, political, religious and racial identity, he depicted the survival of the Jewish people as a fossilized remnant of history, for Jewish particularism does not possess the traits of other 'great' and 'generous' living civilizations, escaping civilizational calls of human intercourse, symbiosis and friendship.[83]

---

[81] Robert Wistrich, *Antisemitism and Multiculturalism: The Uneasy Connection* (Jerusalem: Vidal Sassoon Center for the Study of Antisemitism, Hebrew University of Jerusalem, 2007).
[82] Peter Burke, *Cultural Hybridity* (Cambridge: Polity Press, 2013), p. 9.
[83] Nathan Rotenstreich, *The Recurring Pattern: Studies in Anti-Judaism in Modern Thought* (London: Weidenfeld & Nicolson, 1963), pp. 76-121.

Pessoa, Unknown to Paz

Jerónimo Pizarro

Universidad de los Andes, Colombia

Between 1960 and 1961, Octavio Paz prepared an anthology of Fernando Pessoa's poetry for which he wrote a thirty-page introduction that still today dazzles us for its accuracy and clarity, in spite of the fact that more than fifty years have passed since its publication. The essay 'El desconocido de sí mismo' [A Stranger to Himself] opens the book that has since become a classic: Fernando Pessoa, *Antología* [Anthology], selection, translation and foreword by Octavio Paz (Mexico: Autonomous National University of Mexico, 1962).[1]

This introduction would later be a part of *Cuadrivio* (Mexico: Joaquim Mortiz, 1965), a set of four essays dedicated to Ruben Darío, Ramón López Velarde, Fernando Pessoa and Luis Cernuda, essays that Octavio Paz distributed up until 1990 in different volumes of his *Obras completas* [Complete Works]. Today, 'El desconocido de sí mismo' is found in the second volume of these *Obras*, entitled 'Excursiones / Incursiones — Dominio extranjero' [Excursions / Incursions — Foreign Dominion], preceding a more recent and less-known text: 'Intersecciones y bifurcaciones [Intersections and bifurcations]: A. O. Barnabooth, Álvaro de Campos, Alberto Caeiro', published in the journal *Vuelta*, № 147, in February of 1989. When it was published in the Complete Works, the essay-introduction ended with the words 'París, 1961'; the second text ended 'México, 1988'.

During the preparation of his *Obras completas*, Paz reorganized his books and separated his texts based on Mexican letters ('Generaciones y semblanzas' [Generations and Biographical Sketches]), Hispanic letters ('Fundacion y disidencia' [Foundation and Dissidence]) and other letters ('Excursiones / Incursiones' [Excursions / Incursions]). Fernando Pessoa is mentioned in this last volume, in a chapter on 'Poetas europeos' [European poets], alongside Boris Pasternak, Saint-John Perse, four Swedish poets and Charles Tomlinson. Paz's translations of Fernando Pessoa migrated, without the 1961 essay, to volume VII, 'Obra poética II (1969–1998)' [Poetic Work II, (1969–1998)]. Again, the Portuguese originals of the poems were not included, as Paz argued that his purpose 'was to make, through poems in other languages, poems in mine',[2]

---

[1] A new Mexican reprint (México: UNAM, 2010) now has both names on the cover, Octavio Paz and Fernando Pessoa, and is re-titled *El desconocido de sí mismo. Antología*. See Adolfo Castañón, 'A veces prosa: Pessoa en Paz', *Revista de la Universidad de México*, 79 (2010), 95–97 [also available online].

[2] Octavio Paz, 'Preliminar', in *Obra poética II (1969–1998)*, Obras completas (México: FCE, 2004), pp. 17–18 (p. 17).

thus suggesting that his translations could be read as poems by Octavio Paz. 'My versions', he added, 'do not have philological value, rather, if any, literary and maybe poetic value'; furthermore, he explains, the differences between creation and translation are 'vague'.[3]

In this text, my attention will focus exclusively on Paz's essay, 'El desconocido de sí mismo', leaving out his translations, which deserve a study of their own, given that Pessoa and Paz shared a similar vision of this art. Pessoa mentions, in an aphorism, 'Aquella *reinspiração* sem a qual traduzir é só paraphrasear em outra lingua' [That *re-inspiration* without which translating is but paraphrasing in another language].[4] This concept, 're-inspiration', could have been invented by Paz. In what I am about to lay out, I suggest 'revisiting Pessoa' through the eyes of the Mexican Nobel; remembering Pessoa together with Paz, one of the writers who introduced Pessoa to Latin American readers, even though he discovered Pessoa late, after writing *El arco y la lira: el poema, la revelación poética, poesía e historia* [The Bow and the Lyre: The Poem, the Poetic Revelation, Poetry and History] (1956), a book that discusses, among other things, the European tradition that feeds the poetry written by Hispano-American authors.

* * * * *

'The first time I heard of Fernando Pessoa', writes Paz, 'was in Paris, an autumn night in 1958'.[5] This is an auspicious indication, because we know that it was during these years that Pessoa started to 'trickle' into the Latin American sphere. We lack a panoramic vision of Fernando Pessoa in Latin America, like the one that Antonio Sáez-Delgado has presented about Fernando Pessoa in Spain (2014),[6] but we do know for sure — because he quotes them — that Paz read three Spanish critics, Joaquín de Entrambasaguas, Ángel Crespo and Ildefonso-Manuel Gil, and we can comment on those readings based on what we know about Fernando Pessoa in Spain.

Entrambasaguas published, in 1946, in his *Cuadernos de literatura española* [Journals of Spanish Literature], a bilingual selection of Pessoa's poems, preceded by a study. Gil, in his book *Ensayos sobre poesía portuguesa* [Essays on Portuguese Poetry] (1948), included a long chapter entitled 'La poesía de Fernando Pessoa' [The Poetry of Fernando Pessoa], where he offered 'a Spanish version of the famous letter written to Adolfo Casais Monteiro on the genesis of heteronyms', and where, like Paz, he defended the indestructible unity of

---

[3] Paz, 'Preliminar', p. 17.
[4] BNP/E3, 65-20ʳ. Pessoa's archive (Espólio 3) is housed at the National Library of Portugal (BNP).
[5] Fernando Pessoa, 'El desconocido de sí mismo', in *Antología*, selección, traducción y prólogo de Octavio Paz (México: UNAM, 1962), pp. 11–40 (p. 11).
[6] Antonio Sáez-Delgado, *Pessoa e Espanha* (Lousã: Licorne, 2011); *Pessoa y España* (Valencia: Pre-Textos, 2015). But read Armando Romero, 'Fernando Pessoa en América Latina', *Aleph*, 176 (2016), 62-76, <https://issuu.com/ntcgra/docs/aleph-176>.

Pessoa's work. In 1955, Entrambasaguas published a text of 150 pages, known as *Fernando Pessoa y su creación poética* [Fernando Pessoa and his Poetic Creation]. And finally, in 1958, Crespo wrote an article, 'Fernando Pessoa y sus heterónimos' [Fernando Pessoa and his Heteronyms], for the magazine *Insula*, № 134, of Madrid. Crespo had already published *Poemas de Alberto Caeiro* [Poems of Alberto Caeiro] (Madrid: Adonais, 1957) and he would soon publish in Spain an *Antología de la nueva poesía portuguesa* [Anthology of the New Portuguese Poetry] (Madrid: Rialp, 1961).

These were the main Pessoan publications in Spain at the time. Far away from France, in Argentina, no less, the enthusiastic poet and translator Rodolfo Alonso presented, in 1961, a selection and translation of *Poemas* (Buenos Aires, Fabril Editora) by Fernando Pessoa, poems that he had already published in the magazine *Poesía Buenos Aires*, № 30, in the Spring of 1960. Today we know that Paz and Alonso worked simultaneously, one in Buenos Aires, the other in Paris. In an international conference in Lisbon, Alonso recollected the story of his anthology:

> In late 1959, when I was still young, Aldo Pellegrini (1903–1973) proposed that I should select and translate an ample anthology of Fernando Pessoa, I remember that it was difficult to persuade Francisco Caetano Dias [Pessoa's brother-in-law]. As if his family were ashamed of that strange relative, of life more than anonymous, who kept hidden, under the humble appearance of a sporadic translator of foreign correspondence for commercial houses, the creation of his 'drama em gente' [drama in people] — that multiple creative work that inhabited him.
>
> [...] But the relevant part of this Argentinean novelty (the first publication of the heteronyms in Spanish and the first in Latin America) was not only the publication itself, pioneering in fact, but its intense acclaim in the entire sphere of our language as well. The acceptance of the readers was so immediate that in a short amount of time, without any publicity, it demanded consecutive editions, anticipating what is now obvious: Pessoa captivates his admirers one by one, person by person, through the very potentiality of his poems, without ever being concerned about superficial, planned success and in such an indelible way, that this edition is kept in private libraries as a special event, and in the heart and the memory like a dear friend, a lasting imprint.[7]

Both Alonso's and Paz's anthologies were fundamental to the discovery of Pessoa in the Spanish-language sphere. That is not to say that no one knew Pessoa yet. At least in an incipient way, he was known — Borges mentions Pessoa in a 1963 article, written in collaboration with his friend Alicia Jurado, for the *Enciclopedia práctica Jackson* [Jackson Practical Encyclopedia] [8] — even

---

[7] Rodolfo Alonso, 'Pessoa(s)', II Congreso Internacional Fernando Pessoa, 2010. A shorter and revised version was published in the newspaper *Página 12*: <https://www.pagina12.com.ar/diario/contratapa/13-279276-2015-08-13.html>.

[8] Jorge Luis Borges, 'Portugal: el siglo XX', in *Textos Recobrados, 1956–1986* (Buenos Aires: Emecé, 2003), pp. 56–59. See Patricio Ferrari and Jerónimo Pizarro, 'Borges, Jorge Luis (1899–1986)', in

though only a few had read the author of *Mensagem* [Message], and the family, as Alonso recalls, 'was ashamed' of Pessoa, of 'that strange relative'.

What we know for sure is that Alonso arrived at Pessoa through Aldo Pellegrini, who founded the first surrealist group in South America, and Paz did so through Nora Mitrani, a surrealist author, born in Sofia, who lived in Lisbon and to whom one of the greatest poems of the twentieth century was dedicated, after her return to Paris: 'Um Adeus Português' [A Portuguese Farewell], by Alexandre O'Neill. Mitrani died in 1961, and in honour of her death, Paz wrote, that same year, a few months after her death, 'Nora Mitrani died; I think she would have been happy to know that that discussion in 1958 awoke a passion. That passion is the origin of this little book'.[9] Mitrani brought Paz to Pessoa, she made him read some of her translations in *Le Surréalisme, même* [Surrealism, Itself], and afterwards Paz started to read, just like Émile Cioran,[10] some of Armand Guibert's translations, such as *Poésies d'Álvaro de Campos* [Poetry by Álvaro de Campos] (1944); *Ode maritime* [Maritime Ode] (1955); *Bureau de tabac et autres poèmes* [The Tobacco Shop and Other Poems] (1955); *Ode triomphale et autres poèmes d'Alvaro de Campos* [Triumphal Ode and Other Poems by Alvaro de Campos] (1960); and *Le Gardeur de troupeaux et les autres poèmes d'Alberto Caeiro* [The Keeper of Sheep and Other Poems by Alberto Caeiro] (1960).[11] He also read the essays of Adolfo Casais Monteiro (probably the *Estudos sobre a Poesia de Fernando Pessoa* [Studies of the Poetry of Fernando Pessoa], published in Rio de Janeiro in 1958), received on loan the *Obra Poética* edited by Maria Aliete Galhoz (Rio de Janeiro: Jose Aguilar, 1960), and acquired most, if not all, of the following volumes that Ática published in Lisbon.

>   *Poesias de Fernando Pessoa* [Poetry by Fernando Pessoa] (1942)
>   *Poesias de Álvaro de Campos* [Poetry by Álvaro de Campos] (1944)
>   *Mensagem* [Message] (1945)
>   *Poemas de Alberto Caeiro* [Poems by Alberto Caeiro] (1946)
>   *Odes de Ricardo Reis* [Odes by Ricardo Reis] (1946)
>   *Poemas Dramáticos* [Dramatic Poems] (1952)
>   *Poesias Inéditas (1930-1935)* [Unpublished Poems] (1955)
>   *Poesias Inéditas (1919-1930)* [Unpublished Poems] (1956)

Dicionário de Fernando Pessoa e do Modernismo Português, ed. by Fernando Cabral Martins (Lisbon: Caminho, 2008), pp. 91–92. The 1963 article was published in vol. IX of the *Enciclopedia práctica Jackson: conjunto de conocimientos para la formación autodidacta* (México: W. M. Jackson, 1963), pp. 321–31. See also Daniel Balderston, 'Borges and Portuguese Literature', *Variaciones Borges*, 21 (2006), 157–73 (p. 167): '[there] is evidence of a reading of Pessoa (in the original) by 1960'.

[9] Pessoa, *Antología*, p. 12.

[10] Dagmara Kraus, 'On Pessoa's Involvement with the Birth Theme in Cioran's *De l'inconvénient d'être né*', *Pessoa Plural — A Journal of Fernando Pessoa Studies*, 7 (2015), 23–43 <https://doi.org/10.7301/Z0HD7T5P>. See, in the same journal, Daiane Walker Araujo, 'Octavio Paz, leitor de Fernando Pessoa: crítica, tradução e poesia', 10 (2016), 606–27, also online: <https://doi.org/10.7301/Z01834PW>.

[11] See Anne-Marie Quint, 'Armand Guibert, traducteur de Fernando Pessoa', Lisbon, Atelier du lusitanisme français, Colloque du CREPAL, 23–24 January 2004. Unpublished, but uploaded to this page: <http://www.academia.edu/4071445/Armand_Guibert_traducteur_de_Pessoa>.

All these books, or at least some of them, led Octavio Paz to discover Fernando Pessoa and to write the beautiful and unerring essay, 'El desconocido de sí mismo', in which he defends the idea that: 'We write to be what we are or to be what we are not. In either case we search for ourselves. And if we are lucky enough to find ourselves — a signal of creation — we will discover that we are, in fact, strangers to ourselves'.[12] Paz will find himself through Pessoa, but he too will find another stranger.

* * * * *

One of the most famous utterances in Paz's essay causes us to stop and observe it for a moment: 'Poets don't have biographies. Their works are their biography'.[13] It's a double maxim that the Mexican poet explores again in 1996, two years before his death, within a text that appears to have been written with Pessoa in mind:

> Each poet invents a poet that is the author of his poems. In other words: his poems invent the poet that writes them. The distinction between the epic poet and the lyric poet has always seemed foggy to me. They say that the epic poet — and his descendant: the novelist — recounts outside events and invents characters, while the lyric poet speaks for himself. This is not so: the lyric poet invents himself through the work of his poems. In more than a few cases the idea of 'himself' is composed of a plurality of voices and persons. Like all human beings, the poet is a plural being; from our birth to our deathbed, we live in dialogue — or in dispute — with the strangers that inhabit us. The real biography of a poet is not in the events of his life, but rather in his poems.[14]

On the one hand, it may seem paradoxical that Paz would substitute a poetic biography for a historical one, especially having lead such an eventful life: he lived in various countries, went through many struggles (like the Spanish Civil War), met thousands of authors and artists, was ambassador to Mexico, founded many journals, had more than one marriage, taught classes in many universities (Cambridge, Pittsburgh, Texas at Austin, Cornell and Harvard), clashed with other intellectuals, received countless awards and distinctions, and managed to prepare his *Obras completas*. This in contrast to Pessoa, who after returning from South Africa never left Portugal again, who watched the First World War from afar (as Portugal delayed entering it), did not meet anyone important throughout his life and even tried to avoid an encounter with Aleister Crowley, failed to secure a position as a librarian in Cascais, founded journals that were all ephemeral, who didn't get married and barely had any love interests, who didn't teach classes and wrote critically of the University of Lisbon's professors,

---

[12] Pessoa, *Antología*, p. 22.
[13] Pessoa, *Antología*, p. 12.
[14] Paz, 'Preliminar', p. 18.

won only one award and then of the second order (for *Mensagem*, 1934), was censored by the Salazar dictatorship for insulting the Portuguese dictator — under the pretext that he was defending secret societies — who joked about the Nobel Prize and the possibility of a set of *Obras completas*, and who gathered in just two trunks almost every piece of writing he left for posterity.

But, of course, Paz's position is clear. Even if a writer happened to lead a more than 'tourist' or 'vagabond' life, to use Bauman's words,[15] his life is transmitted, in some measure, in his works. Paz remembers the most 'exceptional' facts about Pessoa's life, but with one caveat: 'provided one recognizes that it is about traces of a shadow. The real Pessoa is other'.[16] It appears that we can retell the story of an individual's life, but only if we acknowledge the illusion — we must direct our attention to the poetry if we want to arrive at the real truth of a life. Naturally, biographers, who tend to flesh out a given figure, would be opposed to this denial of the biography; and certainly Pessoa as an individual is poorly defined, in general, because he, with elegance and class, always wanted to present himself as 'the least there ever was' amidst his heteronyms,[17] as if he hadn't really done anything — an ironic statement by one who did everything.

In an essay entitled 'Phantoms', Paulo de Medeiros writes: 'It is impossible to think about Pessoa without thinking about the spectral character of his figure and of his work'; this is why 'it is always crucial to have a notion as lucid as possible about what can — or must — be designated as Pessoan "ghostliness"'.[18] Medeiros recalls a text by Carlos Queiroz, 'Fernando Pessoa e os seus fantasmas' [Fernando Pessoa and his Phantoms], and 'A Stranger to Himself', by Octavio Paz, who, with a nod to Nietzsche, described Pessoa as the 'taciturn phantom of the Portuguese mid-day'.[19] Medeiros then names other critics that have constructed a 'ghostly' Pessoa and suggests that it is necessary to delve into what we think when we come across a 'ghostly' image of Fernando Pessoa, 'The Man who Never Was', as Jorge de Sena called him.[20]

I believe this is an important point, because Paz appropriates a 'vision' of Pierre Hourcade to respond, indirectly, to an almost impossible question:

---

[15] Zygmunt Bauman, *Liquid Times: Living in an Age of Uncertainty* (Cambridge: Polity Press, 2007).

[16] Pessoa, *Antología*, p. 12.

[17] Fernando Pessoa, *Eu sou uma antologia: 136 autores fictícios*, ed. by Jerónimo Pizarro and Patricio Ferrari (Lisbon: Tinta-da-china, 2013), pp. 641–53. The letter, to his friend Adolfo Casais Monteiro, is translated by Richard Zenith in *The Selected Prose of Fernando Pessoa* (New York: Grove Press, 2001), pp. 251–60.

[18] Paulo de Medeiros, 'Fantasmas', in *O silêncio das sereias: ensaio sobre o 'Livro do Desassossego'* (Lisbon: Tinta-da-china, 2015), pp. 15–31 (p. 15). See also the chapter 'Phantoms and Crypts', in *Pessoa's Geometry of the Abyss: Modernity and 'The Book of Disquiet'* (Oxford: Legenda, 2013), pp. 52–73.

[19] Pessoa, *Antología*, p. 14. Nietzsche claims that a phantom is haunting the modern ego and invokes the ecstatic midday vision experienced by him or Zarathustra. 'Jaspers also points out that Nietzsche's conception of noon or midday is a symbol for the midpoint of the path between man and the Superman'; Richard Lowell Howey, *Heidegger and Jaspers on Nietzsche* (The Hague: Martinus Nijhoff, 1973), p. 154.

[20] *The Man Who Never Was: Essays on Fernando Pessoa*, ed. with an intro. by George Monteiro (Providence, RI: Gávea-Brown, 1982). This includes papers presented at the first International Symposium on Fernando Pessoa, held on 7–8 October 1977 at Brown University.

'Who is Pessoa?' The answer is a confession by Hourcade: 'Never, upon saying goodbye, did I dare to turn my face; I was afraid to see him fade away, dissolved into thin air'.[21] Was Pessoa such an intangible spirit? I do not believe so, and it seems that it was Paz, paradoxically, who left one of the most consistent portrayals of Pessoa, one in which the material and immaterial intermingle well. The portrayal ends with this inquiry:

> Anglomaniac, myopic, courteous, evasive, dressed in dark clothes, reticent and familiar, cosmopolitan who preached nationalism, *solemn investigator of useless things*, never-smiling humorist who chills our blood, inventor of other poets and destroyer of himself, author of paradoxes clear as water and, as water, dizzying: *to fake is to know oneself*, a mysterious man who makes no effort to cultivate mystery, mysterious as the mid-day moon, taciturn phantom of the Portuguese mid-day: Who is Pessoa?[22]

We do not have a biography of Pessoa written by Paz, but he would probably have ended up trying to follow Pessoa's 'phantom' footsteps through the streets of Lisbon, because whether we like it or not, 'the traces of a shadow' always seduce us. We are all phantoms; we all 'phantasize' or indulge in reverie...

* * * * *

Paz writes splendidly that the 'great vice' of Pessoa was the 'imagination'. Shortly thereafter, he attempts an intellectual biography of Pessoa, guided by the influences that Pessoa himself identified in a text to his friend Armando Côrtes-Rodrigues. Paz doesn't say it explicitly — although he places the expression 'Portuguese sub-poets' in quotation marks, which is suggestive — but this is surely the text upon which he developed the biography (probably quoted from a secondary source):

> 1904-1905 — Influencias de Milton e dos poetas inglezes da epoca romantica — Byron, Shelley, Keats e Tennyson. (Tambem, um pouco depois, e influenciando primeiro o *contista*, Edgar Poe.) Ligeiras influencias tambem da escola de Pope. Em prosa, Carlyle. Restos de influências de sub-poetas portuguezes lidos na infancia. — N'este periodo a ordem das influências foi, pouco mais ou menos: (1) Byron; (2) Milton, Pope e Byron; (3) Byron, Milton, Pope, Keats, Tennyson e ligeiramente Shelley; (4) Milton, Keats, Tennyson, Wordsworth e Shelley; (5) Shelley, Wordsworth, Keats e Poe.
>
> 1905 (fim)-1908 — Edgar Poe (já na poesia), Baudelaire, Rollinat, Anthero, Junqueiro (na parte anti-clerical), Cesario Verde, José Duro, Henrique Rosa.
>
> 1908-1909 (fim) — Garrett, Antonio Corrêa d'Oliveira, Antonio Nobre.
>
> 1909-1911 — Os symbolistas francezes, Camillo Pessanha.
>
> 1912-1913 — (1) O saudosismo; (2) Os futuristas.

---

[21] Apud Paz, in Pessoa, *Antología*, p. 14.
[22] Pessoa, *Antología*, p. 14.

[1904–1905 — Influences of Milton and of the English poets from the Romantic era — Byron, Shelley, Keats and Tennyson. (Also, a little later, influenced by Edgar Poe, firstly as *short-story writer*.) Light influences from the Pope school as well. In prose, Carlyle. Residual influences from Portuguese sub-poets read in childhood. — In this period the order of influences was, more or less: (1) Byron; (2) Milton, Pope, and Byron; (3) Byron, Milton, Pope, Keats, Tennyson, and lightly Shelley; (4) Milton, Keats, Tennyson, Wordsworth, and Shelley; (5) Shelley, Wordsworth, Keats, and Poe.

1905 (end)–1908 — Edgar Allan Poe (now the poetry writer), Baudelaire, Rollinat, Antero, Junqueiro (in the anti-clerical part), Cesário Verde, José Duro, Henrique Rosa.

1908–1909 (end) — Garrett, António Correia de Oliveira, António Nobre.

1909–1911 — The French symbolists, Camilo Pessanha.

1912–1913 — (1) Saudosism; (2) The Futurists.]

This text — mainly written by Pessoa[23] — is part of a set of sheets where one can also find some notes taken by Armando Côrtes-Rodrigues, in 1914, and published in the appendix of *Cartas de Fernando Pessoa to Armando Côrtes-Rodrigues* (1945). Those notes about Pessoa include the following:

1901–1902 algumas poesias portuguesas.
1902–1904 tentou escrever romances em ingles.
1904–1908 (setembro) poesia e prosa em ingles.
1908–1914 (poesia, prosa em portugues, ingles e frances)

[1901–1902 some Portuguese poetry.
1902–1904 tried to write stories in English.
1904–1908 (September) poetry and prose in English.
1908–1914 (poetry, prose in Portuguese, English and French)]

These notes corroborate others, according to which, in September of 1908, influenced by the reading of Almeida Garrett and by the patriotism that the João Franco dictatorship inspired in him, Pessoa started to write *predominately* in Portuguese, which had been rare up to then. Paz simply states:

He writes his first poems in English, between 1905 and 1908. At that time, he was reading Milton, Shelley, Keats, Poe. Later he discovers Baudelaire and reads various 'Portuguese sub-poets'. He insensibly returns to his native tongue, although he will never stop writing in English. Until 1912 the influence of symbolist poetry and of 'Saudosism' is preponderant.[24]

It is symptomatic of his general lack of knowledge of Portuguese literature that Paz does not refer by name to a single Portuguese poet — such as Antero de Quental, Cesário Verde or Camilo Pessanha — and only mentions the existence of various 'Portuguese sub-poets'. The truth is that Pessoa admired Quental,

---

[23] The title and some words at the end, '(cartas de M. S. Carneiro)' [Letters by Mário de Sá-Carneiro], were written by Armando Côrtes-Rodrigues. See facsimile in Fig. 1.
[24] Pessoa, *Antología*, p. 14.

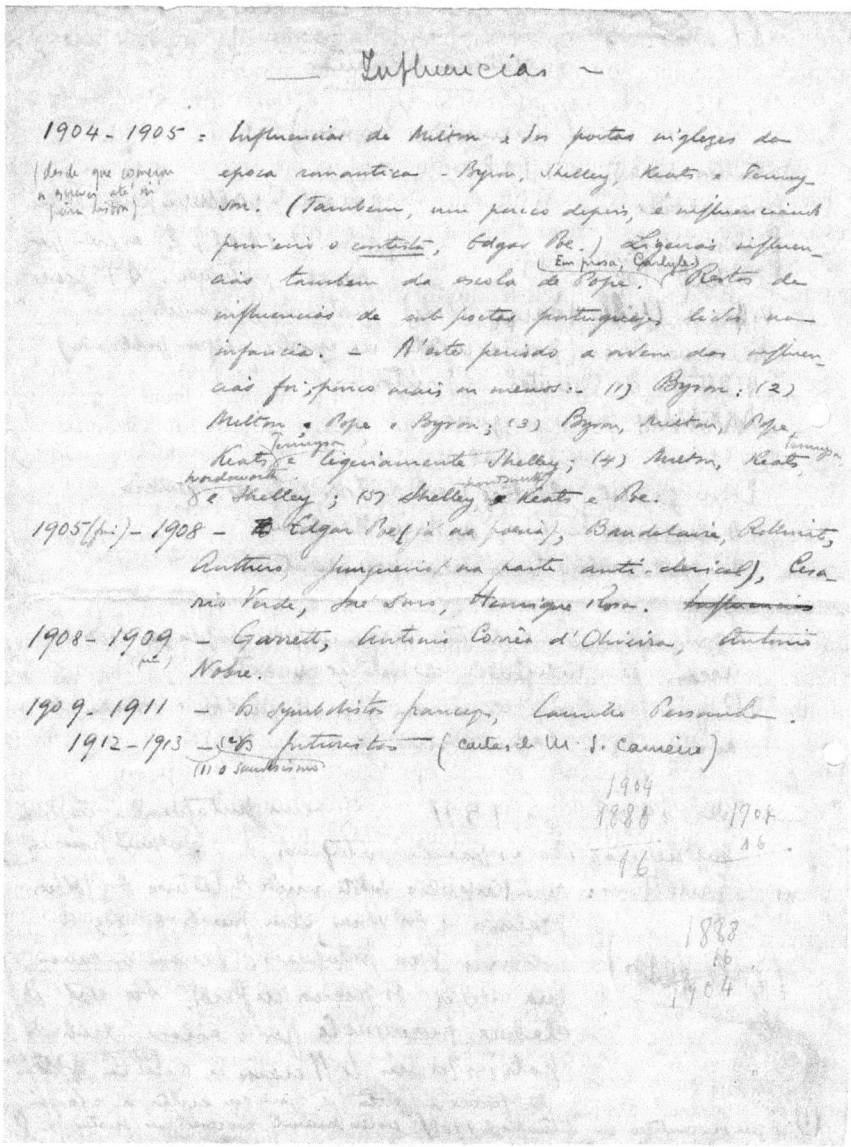

Fig. 1 Note on 'Influences', mostly in Pessoa's own handwriting, reproduced by permission of the holders, the Biblioteca Pública e Arquivo Regional de Ponta Delgada (ACR, n.º 219J).

whom he translated;[25] Verde, to whom he paid homage in *Livro do Desassossego* [The Book of Disquiet];[26] and Pessanha, whom he wanted to publish in *Orpheu*, the most emblematic journal of the first Portuguese modernism. It is very likely that these three poets, in addition to Almeida Garrett and António Nobre, would have determined a turn in the literary production of Fernando Pessoa,[27] who wrote mainly in English until around mid-1908, although he had left South Africa three years earlier. Whitman is missing from the list of names that Pessoa wrote out, but he read him, for the first time, around 1907.[28]

Paz discovers a trilingual poet, but decides, perhaps influenced by other critics, to discount the English and French poets, as well as the author of *Poemas Dramáticos* [Dramatic Poems] (1952). He writes:

> Complex and varied, it moves in different directions: prose, poetry in Portuguese and poetry in English (we will not mention the French poems here, for lack of relevancy). [...] It is not necessary to dwell much on the English poetry; its interest is literary and psychological but does not add much, it seems, to English poetry. The poetic work in Portuguese, from 1902 until 1935, includes *Mensagem*, lyric poetry and dramatic poems. The latter, I believe, have marginal value. Even if they diverge, it remains an extensive poetic work.[29]

Paz senses a discussion that even today has not been settled, and takes sides. The way I see it, he does this because it was only in 2014 that the complete *Poèmes français* were published,[30] whereas the *English Poems* are still largely unpublished today; and the Pessoan *Theatre* is still not widely known.[31] In any case, it is difficult to determine whether Octavio Paz read his play *O marinheiro* [The Sailor], and if he knew how to appreciate it; and it is possible that his assessment of *Poemas dramáticos* (1952) was conditioned by the publication of a misnamed and poorly edited *Primeiro Fausto* [First Faust], a book that was

---

[25] Antero de Quental, *Os Sonetos Completos de Antero de Quental*. With partial English translation by Fernando Pessoa. Preface to Antero de Quental's Sonnets by J. P. Oliveira Martins. Introductory note, transcriptions, and postface by Patricio Ferrari (Lisbon: Ática, 2010).

[26] Jerónimo Pizarro, 'Narciso ciego, iluminado por Lisboa (de Cesário Verde a Fernando Pessoa)', *Abriu — Textuality Studies on Brazil, Galicia and Portugal*, 5 (2016), 35–50 [DOI: 10.1344/abriu2016.5.3].

[27] In his production and in what he considered to be a new literary current around 1912. In an article written that year, Pessoa asserted that the 'distinctive and special tone' of that current began 'with the poem *Só* of António Nobre, with that part of Eugénio de Castro which reminds us of the poetry of the sixteenth century, and with *Os Simples* of Guerra Junqueiro'; it started, thus, 'more or less during the last decade of the nineteenth century' and it had a precursor: Antero de Quental. See Fernando Pessoa, 'Reincidindo', *A Águia*, 2nd series, 5 (May 1912), 137–44. See also Fernando Guimarães, 'A geração do Orpheu e o Simbolismo', in *Simbolismo, modernismo e vanguardas* (Lisbon: Imprensa Nacional–Casa da Moeda, 2004).

[28] Fernando Pessoa [Álvaro de Campos] | Walt Whitman. *Saudação a Walt Whitman | Canto de Mim Mesmo*, ed. by Jerónimo Pizarro; trans. by João Moita (Lisbon: Guerra & Paz, 2017).

[29] Pessoa, *Antología*, p. 35.

[30] Fernando Pessoa, *Poèmes français*, edition established and annotated by Patricio Ferrari in collaboration with Patrick Quillier, preface by Patrick Quillier (Paris: Éditions de la Différence, 2014).

[31] See the introduction to Fernando Pessoa, *Teatro Estático*, ed. by Filipa Freitas and Patricio Ferrari in collaboration with Claudia J. Fischer (Lisbon: Tinta-da-china, 2017).

more thoroughly and completely published in 1988, with the title *Faust*, without any misleading adjective.

Paz's essay deserves all possible praise, but it is also fair to say that Paz does not name any other Portuguese author apart from Fernando Pessoa, and wrote from a Francophone context in which the French and English poems of Pessoa, as well as their Symbolist counterparts (influenced by Belgian, Maeterlinck), had not always been well received. Significantly, Paz redeems Charles Baudelaire, but not Cesário Verde.

* * * * *

Octavio Paz's critical intuitions are multiple and constantly illuminate the essay. He discovers in Pessoa a 'self-absorbed and denying Whitman';[32] he approximates Álvaro de Campos to Barnabooth and Valery Larbaud; he finds defective and incomplete the 'crudely pathological'[33] explanation Pessoa offers about his alleged mental state ('I'm a hysterical neurasthenic'), but he knows that he lives between dispersion and tension and, 'like the great lazy people of our time, he spends his life making catalogues of works he will never write';[34] he takes notice of the absence of women and writes that without that 'central sun [...] the sensible universe vanishes'.[35] His errors — some corrected in later versions — are few: he states that in 1907 Pessoa installed a printing press — it was in 1909; he refers to the painter 'Almada Negreira' — it is Negreiros ; he mentions among a 'fluid mass of imaginary friends' Coelho Pacheco, a 'bad copy of Campos'[36] — because it has only recently been established that Coelho Pacheco was a *real* friend of Fernando Pessoa, and not a semi-being invented by him;[37] and Paz also misspells a few Portuguese words.

But what I wish to redeem now, beyond those great virtues and those minor flaws, and also to close this text, is a critical observation that allows me to link the text of Octavio Paz with another great essay of a twentieth-century Mexican author: 'Machado de La Mancha', by Carlos Fuentes. In 'El desconocido de sí mismo', Paz subtly distinguishes Pessoa from Huidobro ('The poet is not a "little God" but a fallen being').[38] After discussing the rise of *Orpheu*, in 1915, that is to say, the crystallization of the first Portuguese modernism, he observes: 'The amazing thing is the emergence of the group [which was formed around the magazine], ahead of their time and their society. What was being written

---

[32] Pessoa, *Antología*, p. 17.
[33] Pessoa, *Antología*, p. 20.
[34] Pessoa, *Antología*, p. 15.
[35] Pessoa, *Antología*, p. 37.
[36] Pessoa, *Antología*, p. 21.
[37] Maria Aliete Galhoz, 'O Equívoco de Coelho Pacheco', *As mãos da escrita*, ed. by Luiz Fagundes Duarte and António Braz de Oliveira (Lisbon: Biblioteca Nacional de Portugal, 2007), pp. 374–77. See <http://purl.pt/13858/1/>.
[38] Pessoa, *Antología*, p. 17.

in Spain and in Latin America in those years?'[39] And in a footnote a few pages later, he answers: 'In Spanish there was nothing similar until the generation of Lorca and Neruda. There was, indeed, the prose of the great Ramón Gómez de la Serna. In Mexico we had a slow start, only a beginning: José Juan Tablada. In 1918 modern poetry in Spanish language really takes off. But its founder, Vicente Huidobro, is a poet with a very different tone'.[40] Paz understands that *Orpheu* is prior to the Generation of '27, as well as to Surrealism, Dadaism and Ultraism (it actually owes its existence to Futurism, Cubism and perhaps Imagism), and that modern poetry in Portuguese is slightly prior to modern poetry in Spanish. Pessoa, unknown to Paz when he wrote *El arco y la lira* [The Bow and the Lyre] (1956), entered Paz's literary historiography from 1958 onwards, and his essay on Pessoa, finished in 1961 and published in 1962, can be read as a necessary appendix to his study of modern poetry, particularly to the pages devoted to Poetry and History.

That critical intuition, argued by Octavio Paz — that modern poetry in Portuguese is slightly prior to modern poetry in Spanish — leads me to another one, developed by his compatriot Carlos Fuentes. The latter states — in 'Machado de La Mancha', an essay that 'pays unconditional homage' to 'Brazilian writer Machado de Assis, born in 1839 and died in 1908, [...] author of *Memorias Póstumas de Brás Cubas* [The Posthumous Memoirs of Bras Cubas]'[41] — the following:

> [...] I just want to really convey my amazement that in the language of the modern novel founded in La Mancha by Miguel de Cervantes, there has been after *Don Quixote* only fields of solitude and gloomy hills.
>
> *La Regenta*, *Fortunata and Jacinta*, restore vitality to the Spanish novel in Spain and Latin America still must wait, as Spain waited for Clarín and Galdós, and for Borges, Asturias, Carpentier and Onetti.
>
> Instead — and this is the miracle — Brazil gives its nationality, its imagination, its language, to the largest — if not the only — Ibero-American novelist of the past century, Joaquim Maria Machado de Assis.[42]

While Paz recognizes the miracle that is Pessoa, Fuentes does the same for Machado (whose Portuguese brother, so to speak, was Eça de Queiroz). Paz warns that Pessoa is prior to Lorca and Neruda;[43] Fuentes recognizes that Machado restarts a Cervantes tradition that nobody in nineteenth-century Spanish America knew how to recover. 'What did Machado know that Spanish-American novelists did not know? Why the miracle of Machado? The miracle stands on a paradox: Machado assumes, in Brazil, the lesson of Cervantes, the

---

[39] Pessoa, *Antología*, p. 18.
[40] Pessoa, *Antología*, p. 28.
[41] Carlos Fuentes, *Machado de La Mancha* (México: FCE, 2001), p. 5.
[42] Fuentes, *Machado de La Mancha*, p. 9.
[43] In a similar fashion, the curators of the exhibition 'Pessoa: All Art Is a Form of Literature' (Museum Reina Sofia, 7 February — 7 May 2018), admitted that Pessoa's isms were prior to Spanish isms. The catalogue was printed in January 2018.

tradition of La Mancha that has been forgotten by Spanish-American novelists, from Mexico to Argentina, no matter how many civic and scholastic homages that they might have paid to the *Quijote*.[44]

Today, taking advantage of the amazement of these two Mexican writers and their past findings, I would like to close by suggesting three reasons for reading literature written in Portuguese, in addition to strengthening ties between the Spanish and Portuguese languages. These are the following: 1) modern prose and poetry are indebted to great authors who wrote in Portuguese, and some of these authors were able to continue Hispanic traditions better than many other Latin American authors; 2) Pessoa has few contemporary equivalents — Paz mentions Apollinaire and Mayakovsky — and Machado is one of the few strong inheritors, with Laurence Sterne, of Cervantes; 3) precursors frequently write in languages other than their own, and the best readers of their literary tradition tend to be outside of it. Paz did not mention Pessoa in *El arco y la lira*, but today we can read his 'El desconocido de sí mismo' as an addendum to that book and to the general history of modern Ibero-American poetry. Pessoa was unknown to Paz until 1958, but today he is no longer unknown to any great critic of poetry, and Paz is amply responsible for that change. If there is a world literary system, Pessoa is now part of it.

---

[44] Fuentes, *Machado de La Mancha*, pp. 9-10.

Fragmenting Colonial Stereotypes in the Films *Chocolat* (1988) and *Tabu* (2012)

SANDRA RELLIER

University of Minnesota

Introduction

When an explorer at the beginning of Miguel Gomes's film *Tabu* (2012)[1] refers to reality as being a tale, he sheds light on the longing and loneliness of those post-colonial bodies who are still deeply submerged in a former and now forgotten colony.[2] By interpreting reality as a tale, Gomes constructs a space where nostalgia and silence take place in an unknown territory; and where the themes of love, colonialism and guilt are shared within the frameworks of memory and time. Much like what French director Claire Denis, in *Chocolat* (1988),[3] does with her character France, Gomes portrays the archetypes of colonization in the form of a flashback through the life of a woman named Aurora. Both characters in the respective films contribute in different ways to the formation of colonial subjectivities, which are positioned in a time-space external to a colonial period in which memories are constructed and commonly stereotyped. The flashbacks are essential in negotiating memories of colonial history after a time of colonialism. For Bhabha, the stereotyped others are usually portrayed as excess; they remain ambivalent objects of desire and often stay within marginalized spaces.[4] Both Denis and Gomes expose this excess by revealing their characters' colonial marginalization as being anything but the norm. Rather, they each take those marginalizations and make them the focus of their respective films to reach both a recognition and a transformation of the stereotype. This also reveals both colonial and post-colonial commonalities among former empires that have yet to be compared on a larger scale, for little scholarship exists confronting French and Portuguese colonial empires.[5]

---

[1] *Tabu*, dir. by Miguel Gomes (O Som e a Fúria, Komplizen Film, Gullane Filmes, 2012).
[2] Throughout this article I often refer to the former colonials as belonging to the post-colonial ontology of the former metropolis.
[3] *Chocolat*, dir. by Claire Denis (Orion Classics, 1988).
[4] Homi Bhabha, 'The Other Question: Difference, Discrimination, and the Discourse of Colonialism', in *The Location of Culture* (London and New York: Routledge, 2004), pp. 94–120.
[5] See for example, Alexander Keese, *Living with Ambiguity: Integrating an African Elite in French and Portuguese Africa, 1930–61* (Stuttgart: Steiner, 2007). In this study, Keese offers a comparison of the two empires, in regards to the rhetoric of assimilation as well as the idea of 'benign paternalism' during the 1950s. Another example is the European Research Council funded project MEMOIRS, which is currently led by Margarida Calafate Ribeiro and hosted at the Center for Social Studies, in Coimbra,

In that vein, this article uses commonplaces of postcolonial theory and of feminist theory to question 'what post-colonial?' and examines the norm of excess, which condemns the silenced Other. While Denis directly presents her film from a female viewpoint named France, Gomes strategically hides from view the male narrator of Aurora's story, Ventura, after initially showing him evoking the past soon after he is informed that Aurora has died. The fact that in that scene he is sitting in a bright sunny room in the home for the elderly where he lives signals the clarity of his vision into the past. His (male) voice is that perspective, one that is so naturalized in Western culture as to be confused with the woman's voice and vision. Put differently, Gomes shows how the man represents Aurora's viewpoint by appropriating what is supposed to be her voice, her viewpoint. This article considers both the technique of the flashback and these two viewpoints to demonstrate the possibility of the unfixity of the stereotyped. Both *Chocolat* and *Tabu* are clear representations of the fluidity of memory within a discourse of colonial fixity that defines, through repetition, the boundaries of the stereotyped, presented as different and not belonging to the colonial norm.[6] They both embrace the technique of the flashback in a way that challenges the problematic of the 'colonized Other' in discourses of colonialism and post-colonialism.

While a significant amount of scholarship on Denis's film, *Chocolat*, has been produced since its release in 1988, scholarship on Gomes's *Tabu* (2012) only began to emerge in the past few years. Some of this scholarship includes works by Susan Hayward, Cornelia Ruhe and Levilson Reis, in the case of *Chocolat*, and Paulo de Medeiros and Ana Cristina Pereira for *Tabu*. All this scholarship explores, to some degree, how the directors expose the colonial, racial and gendered relations that build different subjectivities virtually erased from colonial memories. When Ruhe argues that Denis constructs a colonial situation that reflects the unknown effects of colonialism, such as those on personal relations, she echoes Albert Memmi's idea that colonialism affected not only the colonized but also the colonizer.[7] Additionally, in reference to *Tabu*, Paulo de Medeiros and Ana Cristina Pereira raise the question of the major after-effect of colonialism on the post-colonial bodies of the colonized but also of the colonizer, as these bodies are not dead. Rather, they assert that there are insuperable memories, which are usually associated with the nouns 'nostalgia' and 'loss'.[8] These scholars recognize the cultural and historical complexities that, to this day, do not seem to be acknowledged in colonial and post-colonial theory. All these scholars show that it is possible to re-interpret

Portugal. This project aims to re-conceptualize the colonial legacy as part of a European identity.
[6] Bhabha, p. 95.
[7] Cornelia Ruhe, 'Beyond Post-colonialism? From *Chocolat* to *White Material*', in *The Films of Claire Denis: Intimacy on the Border*, ed. by Marjorie Vecchio (London and New York: I. B. Tauris, 2014), pp. 111–24 (p. 111).
[8] See also Susan Hayward, 'Claire Denis' Films and the Post-Colonial Body — with special reference to Beau travail (1999)', *Studies in French Cinema*, l (2001), 159–65 (p. 160).

the colonial period from different perspectives, as demonstrated by Denis and Gomes in their films, which are, for Pereira, a way to re-consider the processes of identifying and deconstructing alterity in colonial discourse.[9] In her work, Hayward questions to whom the post-colonial period belongs.[10] In doing so, she attempts to discuss how the relationships among the characters in the film *Chocolat* begin from a colonial discourse that can also be seen beyond the clichés of colonial encounters. Her argument, like Pereira's, raises questions about the colonial commonalities among post-colonial populations,[11] such as those represented in these two films.[12] Synopses of the films are in order before their respective analysis.

Produced in 1988 and directed by Denis, the film *Chocolat* is set in colonial French Cameroon and tells the story of a French family. Marc and Aimée Dalens are the parents of a young girl, France, who befriends a household servant and Cameroon native man named Protée. The film starts by presenting France as an adult woman walking down a road in Cameroon until an African-American man, William, and his son pick her up. As she rides along in their car, her mind drifts away, and takes the audience on a journey into her childhood and her life as the daughter of a colonial administrator. The rest of the film — save for the last minute — is presented through her perspective, highlighting both her friendship with Protée and the sexual tension between him and her mother, Aimée. This tension is made evident upon the arrival of Luc Segalen, a Western drifter, who ends up staying with the family and fighting with Protée because of Aimée's attraction for him. After the fight, which Aimée witnesses without their knowledge, Aimée attempts to seduce Protée. His rejection of her advances results in him losing his position as a household servant, and he is assigned to the garage. The end of the film presents France, her parents and local black people witnessing the departure of another white family. This scene is enough for the audience to surmise that France and her family will be subjected to the same fate. It also leads the audience progressively back to France's life as an adult, on the road with William and his son. The end of the film then proceeds to position France as an adult observer of what appears to be day-to-day life in post-colonial Cameroon.

Gomes mirrors Denis's narrative by placing his film in a colonial/post-colonial Portuguese context. In his 2012 film, *Tabu*, which takes place in an

---

[9] Ana Cristina Pereira, 'Alteridade e identidade em *Tabu* de Miguel Gomes', *Comunicação e Sociedade*, 29 (2016), 311–30 (p. 311).

[10] Susan Hayward, 'Reading Masculinities in Claire Denis's *Chocolat*', *New Cinemas: Journal of Contemporary Film*, 1 (2002), 120–27 (pp. 121–23).

[11] In post-independence wars, these populations are respectively identified as the *pieds-noirs*, in France, and the *retornados*, in Portugal. However, in the case of Denis's film it is important to note that these populations are from Cameroon and are not identified as *pieds-noirs*.

[12] See Phil Hoad's article in which at the end he refers to both directors as tackling similar issues in colonial Africa. 'Colonialism on film: how cinema finds new ways to bust an old Tabu', *The Guardian*, 26 March 2013, <https://www.theguardian.com/film/filmblog/2013/mar/26/colonialism-on-film-tabu> [accessed 23 June 2017].

undefined place and time in colonial Africa, he tells the story of Aurora, a white Portuguese woman, in two sections, 'Paradise Lost' and 'Paradise'. As an introduction to these sections, Gomes starts with a 'Prologue', which, in voice-over, tells a poetic legend about a beautiful woman who has a mysterious empathy for a sad crocodile. The first section, 'Paradise Lost', directly follows the 'Prologue' and introduces a woman, Pilar, who appears to be worried about the declining health of her neighbour, Aurora, whose maid, Santa, shares this concern. Aurora is shown at a casino, presumably the Casino Estoril, blaming her maid's knowledge of voodoo for her losing money. Soon after, she is hospitalized in a state of confusion and realizes that she is getting closer to death; she tells Pilar and Santa that she feels that someone is missing in her life and calls out the name, 'Gian Luca Ventura'. She wants Pilar to find him, but she dies before he appears on the scene. This man becomes the narrator of the next section, 'Paradise', which takes the audience back to Aurora's early life, shortly before the Portuguese colonial wars began.[13] In Portuguese Africa, Aurora and her husband live near the Tabu Mountain and Aurora is shown to be a skilled hunter, and the owner of a small crocodile that her husband has given her as a gift. One day her crocodile escapes, and Aurora finds it in the house of a man called Ventura. After this encounter, a passionate love affair develops between the two, which is explored in the form of a silent movie. However, when Ventura confides to his friend and band leader, Mário, about the affair, Mário asks him to end it. When Aurora and Ventura do not comply, Mário fights Ventura and a heavily pregnant Aurora picks up a gun and shoots Mário. After she gives birth, her husband comes to pick her up, and Ventura leaves Africa soon after.

Approaching the Feminized and Racialized Other

This article critically reads Laura Mulvey's notion of the feminized Other and Homi Bhabha's notion of the racialized Other. Bhabha describes 'Otherness' through the notion of fixity as well as the idea that a social thought has not evolved throughout time. According to Bhabha, the fixity of the Other results in a paradoxical mode that 'connotes rigidity and an unchanging order as well as disorder, degeneracy and daemonic repetition'.[14] The paradox of the fixed and the repeated stereotype demonstrates that this Other theoretically stays 'in place' while moving in time and maintains this Other's marginalization while exceeding societal norms. In turn, this marginalization is what leads to the stereotyping of the Other, something that sets a clear cultural barrier between the stereotyped and non-stereotyped, where the stereotyped is unable to escape and becomes the excess. In fact, this suggests that, in order to change a society, there must be a recognition of this marginalization of the one who is

---

[13] The Portuguese colonial war first began in 1961 in Angola and was followed by Guiné Bissau in 1963 and Mozambique in 1964.
[14] Bhabha, p. 94.

known to be the Other in colonial discourse. Laura Mulvey does not refer to the stereotyped other per se, but through her interpretation of the male gaze she hints at a feminized stereotype. Specifically, through an analysis of the cinematic text, she explains that the female body is constructed by, through, and for men. These three viewpoints are not only what constitute the male gaze but also consequently leave no space for female agency, as this female subject is dehumanized and left to be consumed by the audience as a spectacle of fascination and male phantasy. The woman in Mulvey's analysis is not the bearer of the gaze, but rather the object that causes the fixity of the male gaze and the stereotyped female body.

To be sure, this article intends to demonstrate that Mulvey's and Bhabha's theoretical truth claims on the racial and feminine stereotypes have contributed to the formation of post-colonial fixities: first, the fixity of the male gaze and second, the fixity of the colonial stereotype. Denis's and Gomes's films clearly break these fixed notions by using flashbacks, as these enable post-colonial self-identifications. These flashbacks allow, specifically, for a self-identification of the female colonial character to occur, because the female story — notwithstanding its implicit male manipulation in Gomes's *Tabu* — is by the end recovered. Thus, like Hayward, who takes the post-colonial 'body as an embodiment of the post-colonial event/moment',[15] this article interprets the flashbacks of female post-colonial bodies to make silenced colonial moments/events tangible. Since, the women protagonists, namely France (*Chocolat*) and Aurora (*Tabu*), become the focus in both the colonial and post-colonial discourses, fluidity of the otherwise stereotyped Other is possible in these films. In this case, fragmentation of the fixed Other can only occur when colonial subjectivities, that is the racial or feminine other, are placed in the present outside of their personal colonial discourse. As a result, with and in these flashbacks, the directors are able to show their colonial suffering as well as alienation after the end of colonization.

Re-imagining the Colonial Other

Both Denis and Gomes illustrate in their films via flashback the way in which colonial fixity is formed, meaning that the stereotyped Other is placed outside of the colonial norm and subsequently loses his/her agency. Thus, in one way, the Other then becomes stereotyped; in another way, by exposing this stereotyping within a specific time-space via flashbacks, Denis and Gomes have the Other represent a different colonial period. The traditionally stereotyped, who has remained ambivalent throughout time, is the one who gains a type of control over this colonial period. The Other or, the excess subject, holds the key to the unknown past where he is a product of economic discourse, power and domination.[16] It is precisely for these reasons that it is essential to unfix the ideas

---

[15] Hayward, 'Claire Denis' Films', p. 160.
[16] Bhabha, p. 96.

of both the racial Other and the male gaze that objectify and hence 'colonize' the woman. In Other words, these films also depict memories that have been silenced within colonial and post-colonial discourses. Thus, for fluidity of the stereotyped as well as social recognition to occur, colonial binaries also need to be broken as these contribute to their fixed construction. The present article adds to Hayward's argument concerning Denis's refusal of Western binaries.[17] These may be understood as the stereotyping of the racialized and feminized Other. For this reason, while it is evident that these binaries, identified by Bhabha as subjectification, are present in *Chocolat* and *Tabu*, they must also remain within the spectrum of the colonial past and be accepted in the post-colonial period. The flashbacks become even more essential in breaking these binaries. In fact, unlike Lacan's 'mirror stage', the colonial woman first shown within a post-colonial time is confronted, through the flashbacks, with a different colonial reality and wakes up from a lifetime of misrecognition.[18] Therefore, in the films, it is the female post-colonial adult who recognizes herself, either directly or through mediation, in colonial discourse. In the end, she defies the fixity imposed by the Man identified in Laura Mulvey's theory as the one who controls the 'female phantasy'.[19]

The gaze that for Laura Mulvey controls the female body seems to disappear in Denis's and Gomes's films by being presented from the direct or indirect point of view of each film's female protagonist. Each woman, Aurora and France, appears to challenge the male gaze not only because she defies the norm of excess in the flashback, but also because the colonial woman/girl has or is given a freedom of movement. This is shown in *Chocolat* in two ways: first, through the protagonist's name, France; and, second, through the camera angles shot mainly from her point of view. The decision to name the protagonist France gives her more authority, as shown when, after Protée is being read a letter out loud, France calls out for him and tells him it is time to go home. In this scene not only does Protée, the servant, oblige her demand, but they are both followed by a crowd of other children. Her authority is also emphasized when Protée calls her 'Boss lady'; but what breaks the racial and feminized fixity here is the play with camera angles as, after putting her in a position of authority, Denis switches camera angles to show Protée as an equal from France's perspective, meaning that when he comes towards her, he comes straight at her rather than from a downward angle. Mulvey's gaze is thus defied not only through France, as the bearer of the gaze, but also through Denis's careful use of facial close-up and France's neutral facial expression. In the end, these filmic choices show the director's intention to revisit the past and challenge the power relations of colonial discourse.

---

[17] Hayward, 'Claire Denis' Films', p. 160.
[18] Laura Mulvey 'Visual Pleasure and Narrative Cinema', in *Visual and Other Pleasures* (London: Palgrave Macmillan, 1989), pp. 14–26 (p. 20).
[19] Mulvey, p. 19.

Similarly, in *Tabu*, Gomes defies the norm of excess by exposing his main character's adultery. Indeed, throughout these adulterous scenes Aurora shows her happiness and subsequently demonstrates her ability to gain control of her own body. Gomes gives her a type of freedom that is usually denied to women, as shown in the scenes with her husband, for Aurora appears to be quieter. However, that fixity is broken when Aurora and her lover clearly continue their relationship, even after Mário warns them to end it. The numerous adulterous scenes, Aurora's killing of Mário, and Aurora's last words in her letter, where she admits she loved him, defy Mulvey's gaze. Aurora not only kills a man but also embodies a woman who found love with a man other than the white soldier. Thus, despite the difficulty they face and their being separated in the end, their affair gives them an unexpected authority that challenges the feminized stereotype. Like France, Aurora represents an Other, who via flashback defies power relations imposed by colonial and post-colonial discourses.

The Silenced Other

By illustrating colonial relations from a different perspective, that is, through the direct and indirect point of view of women, the directors demonstrate that they understand how indispensable it is to reframe colonial discourse. As seen in both films, not only are binaries like colonized/colonizer, woman/man, and civilized/uncivilized exposed, but they also go beyond them by revealing other types of interactions that both challenge the norm and represent the excess. They accomplish this by using the idea of a silenced colonial stereotype, where the 'silenced' in this case depicts the excess. In fact, the latter reveals the unseen: the situations, sites and people, which were part of the protagonists' memory. In *Chocolat*, one can observe this revelation and the fragmenting of colonial discourse through the relationship seen and shared in France's flashback of her relationship with the black servant, called Protée, during her childhood. This childhood relationship breaks the fixity, revealing the complexity of Protée's personal story as much as it allows France to answer some of her unresolved questions from her childhood in Africa, like why Protée left the house. Through the memory, displayed via flashback, one learns that he did not leave because he misbehaved, but rather due to France's mother, Aimée, another white woman.[20] He leaves because of the silenced interactions that he had with Aimée and her inability to resist him. This segment exposes the colonial woman's reality of straddling the line between being white and being a woman, meaning that she belonged to the colonial norm, while still being in an inferior position to the military white male. It is this process of self-reflection and revelation of secrecy that challenges colonial discourse.

[20] This motif appears in Ferdinand Oyono's *Une Vie de Boy* (1956), which for Ruhe exposes the colonizer as subject of many onlookers' 'gaze', such as their domestic servants. These onlookers, she states, know the colonizer's every move and thus challenge the power relations in colonial discourse (Ruhe, 'Beyond Post-colonialism?', p. 113).

When Denis and Gomes challenge the place of the silenced Other in relation to the colonial norm by revealing the unseen, they create a different colonial discourse. In a scene where Protée is put in the foreground one can see him shower and cry in silence while Aimée walks into her house with her daughter, France. This scene defies colonial discourse by the simple fact that the black man is revealed suffering in silence, subsequently showing the reality of colonial oppression that condemns the black servant to silence both his emotions and desires. This scene reveals the colonial intensity between the colonized and the colonizer, while also highlighting the idea of colonial excess as Denis draws attention, in this close-up, to his black body. Indeed, this one puts forward the black man, the racialized Other, as outside the norm that is represented by the white mother. However, what eventually breaks Bhabha's fixity are the emotions expressed by the black man as well as the fact that he is put in the foreground in the image, physically placing him in front of France and Aimée and, thus, psychologically highlighting his emotional distress. This close-up, showing the reality of the Other and the colonial reality of the white woman in the background, challenges the respective stereotypes of white master/servant boy.

This scene is an example of hybridization, as for Ruhe hybrid people are 'trapped between one or more cultures, confronted with problems of alienation and non-belonging'.[21] Specifically, hybridity is created when Protée's facial emotions clearly show the sentiment of non-belonging, for he is shown as being literally cut from the house, forced to shower outside. He is alienated from another culture that is represented by both the mother and her daughter as much as the house in the background. While he is alienated from the household in this scene, his silenced emotions show his inner struggle with his situation as regards the mother and the daughter. Additionally, colonial discourse is fragmented through the complex relations and interactions between the protagonists, which remain indirect and silenced, thus demonstrating to the audience the norm of excess while still breaking it: the woman fulfils her role as a mother but the black man's body is the primary focus of the scene, which may leave the audience perplexed in front of their colonial social roles (the servant and the mother).

As for Gomes, he contributes to that black/white revelation of memory interaction by focusing most of his film on the interactions between two white characters. It is adultery that is Aurora's secret memory, and it is the persistence of this memory, coupled with the audience's knowledge of the latter, that defies colonial discourse. This adultery, that she indirectly asks for on her deathbed, is seen as a form of treason towards her husband, a white colonial military man, as he is higher in rank compared to her lover, Ventura, a musician and member of a band who is, theoretically, loyal to Aurora's husband. While her husband who, for Mulvey, would control the movements and actions of the woman, represents

[21] Ruhe, p. 117.

the fixed 'I', Ventura's relationship with Aurora and his decision to narrate this relationship symbolizes and challenges the fixed white and privileged identity depicted in colonial discourse.[22] Furthermore, the decision to show this memory as a flashback and in the form of a silent movie leaves room for words and actions of truth.[23] The silence gives the opportunity for the post-colonial audience, as well as the post-colonial body, to express itself through actions that were once quieted (still quieted) under the hegemonic colonial discourse. This reveals how the silenced memories depicted through the sites, situations and the people expose the colonial norm of excess in the present post-colonial by including the audience, and potentially changing their point of view. The directors seem to transport their present post-colonial audience back in time, via these flashbacks, to engage the audience and create a new relationship between characters and gender/racialized roles in society — a relationship that revolves around the colonial experiences of the Other that speak for themselves, rather than being spoken for through fixed stereotyped images.

Speaking Bodies and the Deconstruction of Excess

Pereira explains that the silencing of the 'Other' is used to emphasize the positivity and superiority of the 'I' and the 'norm'.[24] However, by giving voice to these silenced bodies, the directors of these films question the helplessness and silencing, frequently associated with the stereotypes of the racialized and feminized bodies. Thus, the Other body becomes the post-colonial voice which breaks the image of helplessness. This image enables both directors to show how the Other body, black and feminine, is stuck in the time when authority came from the fixed 'I', as in the white male. The silenced body, that is, Bhabha's 'excess', is the one that cannot talk openly but tells its story by defying and showing the fixity that the Other experienced. This is illustrated when Alison Murray describes Denis's depiction of Protée's black body as 'glistening with sweat or soapy water [...] sensuously revealed by the camera on numerous occasions'.[25] The scene in which Protée showers outside and away from the white person's view exposes the other black man as one body that is not only racialized and hypersexualized, but also clearly shown as being 'excess' to white society. He becomes a sexual excess that may provoke desire in the white woman, yet he remains outside the norm, as he is shown outside the household. Denis exposes Protée in such a way that his body is purposely positioned by a close-up that shows his sexuality, to provide a certain visual pleasure, that

---

[22] Mulvey, p. 20.
[23] The term 'truth' here to refers to the idea that the flashback reveals the events that have been hidden until the present moment. When the flashback starts, and takes the audience into colonial Africa, these events are finally revealed to the public eye and thus expose a different kind of truth.
[24] Pereira, p. 328.
[25] Alison Murray, 'Women, Nostalgia, Memory: *Chocolat, Outremer,* and *Indochine*', *Research in African Literatures*, 33 (2002), 235–44 (p. 240).

Aimée herself never has the pleasure to enjoy. Denis, in other words, uses the image of the black body as excess to challenge colonial desire and its boundaries as this one shot exposes the black body by presenting the trappings of colonial authenticity from a different perspective.

Along with that scene, *Chocolat* includes multiple other examples of images that illustrate the excess. For example, when the young France stumbles upon a grotesque scene with dead animals, it is Protée who bends down over these dead animals to try and make sense of the destruction. Initially viewed through France's eyes, this scene can break boundaries and assumptions with France's facial expression when the camera angle shifts from France's point of view to Protée's, demonstrating, in essence, a double helplessness through France's inability to understand the destruction and Protée's instinct to try and understand the situation by remaining silent and staring at France. This means that Denis's choice to position Protée in the middle of the animals identifies him with these animals, and almost transforms him into one of them, while, at the same time, France becomes the symbol of authority through her gaze. Conversely, the change in angle breaks these fixed stereotypes, as Denis does not leave room for the audience to identify with one or the other, by making them both subjects of the destruction. It almost seems as if Denis is seeking for the post-colonial audience to disengage from the girl, as the daughter of a colonizer, by later showing, through Protée's perspective, France's facial expression of disgust in front of the horrific scene. In the end, what creates an effect of excess in the scene is the uneasy interaction happening between the two characters, surrounded by dead animals. Their mutual uneasiness hinders any possibility of an I, since neither is given a true role of authority. Both, and not just Protée, subsequently become a part of the gruesome scene rather than reiterating the distinction between the colonizer and colonized. For Pereira, in *Tabu*, the different Other is characterized both culturally, such as when the older Aurora accuses her maid of being a witch, and racially. This racialized Other is indirectly seen in Ventura's narrative and the images showing the black people, often present in the background.[26] For instance, the helpless and submissive body appears when Aurora is first seen hunting and the black servants are shown heads down, working in the fields. This portrayal of the black man as part of the hunting ground illustrates the idea of being black as being inferior and comparing it to an animal, for no real animal is seen next to the black workers in the scene; of black as an excess in colonial society and particularly in a colonial African society. In addition, the racialized excess is fragmented when, in another hunting scene, the black workers are witnessing Aurora hunting. When she leaves the scene, the shot focuses on the black workers and the narration goes on to explain how after this, she was done hunting. This scene precedes her first act of adultery and the introduction to the militia's uprising. Thus, it seems Gomes compares Aurora's secret to the uprising of the

[26] Pereira, p. 325.

militias, to show the existence of a defiance of colonial stereotypes.

The directors play with the image of the excess in their depictions within the post-colonial framework. While the excess in post-colonial discourse in both films is illuminated by a feminized body that is depicted as emotionally lost and in a transitory space, each director also portrays a controversial image of the woman. The depiction of the post-colonial body as excess forces the characters, in the present, to attempt to reconcile with the past, which can only be done by un-silencing and re-discovering a hidden past. For both female protagonists, only by going back to a time seen as happy can they rediscover their realities and the reasons they became the women they are in the post-colonial time. In the case of Aurora in *Tabu*, for example, the audience realizes that the flashback shows a strong and 'happy' woman, as seen throughout her many encounters with Ventura. This flashback hence contrasts with her existence in the present as an insane old woman. While it may be argued that Aurora loses agency, given that her story is told by Ventura, a male and her lover, this article attempts to fragment this argument by acknowledging that Aurora asks for her lover to re-appear in her life, thus, in a way, controlling the gaze that is bestowed upon her in the flashback. She summons the one person who not only knows her truth but who will also be able to tell her true love story. As Gomes explains in an interview, 'A segunda é quase uma sessão de espiritismo: falar com o passado é quase como falar com mortos' [the second is almost a spiritualist séance: to speak with the past is almost like speaking with the dead], which gives Aurora voice and, consequently challenges, to some extent, the male gaze in both discourses (asking for him and her death enabling a discussion of her past).[27]

This 'truth', revealed through the flashback, took her out of a trapped life, which her death allows her to escape, and find freedom like she had, in Africa, with her lover, Ventura. Her decision to commit adultery in the past, and her need to make sense of her life, by returning to this past as an adult via her lover, is visible through her facial expressions, illustrated through smiles and the feeling of exuberance often, if not only, visible during the flashbacks. She was liberated despite being trapped in an unhappy married life, as shown through her secret interactions with Ventura (even when her husband was present), and having her desires socially silenced. Her happiness was silenced and she was silent as the woman, since she did not have the right to express herself. In fact, in one of the moments when she narrates the story, Aurora herself explains in a letter to Ventura that her life outside of her love affair is a life of innocence, a life of nobility in which her escapades do not exist, as these are unfortunately not moments of reality. Applying Mulvey's theory, this means she sees herself as an 'indispensable element of spectacle'.[28] Aurora is at first left without the

---

[27] João Maria Mendes and Jorge Leitão Ramos, 'Sobre dois filmes: *Tabu* de Miguel Gomes e *Deste lado da ressurreição* de Joaquim Sapinho; Entrevista com António Reis e Margarida Cordeiro' (Amadora: Escola Superior de Teatro e Cinema, 2013), p. 9.
[28] Mulvey, p. 19.

possibility to develop the main narrative, but through her adultery, with the non-military musician, she expands this fixed vision of the emotional and immobile woman. She becomes and creates her own narrative, which exposes and raises the question of fluidity within feminine silenced memories. Put another way, she deconstructs the image of excess that was/is bestowed upon her as the wife of a white military man.

Spatial and Temporal Mobility: The Other's Gaze

The fixity of the racialized and feminized body is broken when the stereotyped body has access to spatial and temporal mobility in a colonial territory. This aspect of moving bodies and, to some extent, memories, throughout time and space fragments Bhabha's idea of fixity. This is shown in *Chocolat* through a permanent mark, a burn, on France's hand that she gets by following Protée into the boiler room. When she asks him if the pipes will burn her, he answers by touching the pipes, to which she responds by also touching the pipes and yelling, because it hurts. His unconventional answer to her question, made in silence, may initially shock the audience, but it is this burn that identifies the girl to the audience in both the colonial and the post-colonial sections of the film. In fact, through this burn the audience officially discovers France's identity, as both the girl and the young woman in the car. As a result, it is the burn that confirms that those are her memories, that she is/was the colonial girl introduced to the audience. This burn shows the audience the true relation she had with Protée, the servant, as she gets burnt under and because of his silence. His unconventional way of literally teaching the girl a lesson makes that memory impactful. This permanent mark may represent the colonial discourse through time but it is the post-colonial body that has the possibility to break and fragment the fixity of the permanent, installed here physically and psychologically in the adult France. In other words, by making the scene of the burn and Protée leaving the boiler room her last colonial memory, the stereotype of the racialized other is broken, as the black man is given the choice to leave. As for the girl, her permanent mark fragments fixity by remaining as a memory associated with a black man, thus exposing how the relations between the black man and the girl are the unfixed and the unseen, which at the same time, moves away from Bhabha and Mulvey's truth claims.

Furthermore, by using Protée's image as both servant and friend, Denis challenges both Bhabha's and Mulvey's theoretical notions. She does so, first by giving this black servant authority on multiple occasions and, second by putting forth the life of a young girl and a black man. Unlike what Mulvey would describe as the male gaze and its ability to control movements, Denis depicts Protée, a man, as a type of teacher. One example can be found in the scene when he teaches the girl how to name parts of the body in his native language. This scene challenges colonial discourse, that they are both subjected to at the time, by revealing the role of the servant within the French family's household, which is regularly associated with the maid. Likewise, the scene when little France burns her hand is the most significant in terms of body memory because it is one of the last scenes in the film in which the audience sees the colonial period. This burn is the key to understanding the importance of the flashback as she goes back to her childhood territory without revealing the exact location of Douala, the place for which she is looking. Instead, while in William's car, the audience is shown Cameroon's landscape and day-to-day life. So, if this burn present on her body is permanent, it also allows the story of both the black servant and the girl to emerge and mix. This is a crucial scene in the film narrative in that it illuminates both the physical and psychological marks that remain on France after colonialism.

In *Tabu*, Gomes, once again, shows the unfixed image of bodies through the memory of the adulterous relationship between Aurora and Ventura. The control of their own bodies appears to be the only form of control they can exercise within their social lives in colonial society. This is because they are both seen, albeit at different levels, as lower in rank in comparison to Aurora's husband, who is part of the Portuguese military. When Aurora and Ventura are together, shot in fragmentary scenes in the second section of the film, Mulvey's concept of spectacle is defied. This is because Aurora is portrayed as more than just a vision made for, by and through men. She moves from being happy, during her adventures with Ventura, to passivity as a colonial wife. Gomes's use of stereotyped bodies in a silent movie perhaps can be read as an intentional decision to allow the audience to feel empathy or simply understand her truth and the secret memories that, eventually, do identify her. These memories are the person she really is but who has been forced to hide as an adult in the post-colonial time. She dies with these silenced memories still trapped within her, while her dead body manages to live, via flashback, the life she would have wanted to have in her real post-colonial life. The narrated flashback gives Aurora permission to move from one memory to another, from one reality to another, meaning that the narration of her reality exposes her existence as a stereotyped but defying woman in both discourses. The flashback shows that by using this woman and her body (typically seen as sensual, sexual, etc.), there is a possible presence of a fixity of colonial discourse, since she becomes a vehicle for the stereotyped gendered and racialized colonial body. Her mobility, through the flashback, allows her to tell her story in a post-colonial time, and that challenges the male patriarchal gaze in principle illustrated by Aurora's husband.

Conclusion

As aforementioned, to refer to colonial fixity is to interpret colonial discourse through the lenses of those who do the stereotyping rather than those who are stereotyped. In this respect, both Denis and Gomes negotiate the fixity by reducing the role of the colonial male gaze. It is not by chance that throughout the films the military husbands are so seldom seen. Reducing their roles within a discourse that stands external to a temporal fixity sets a different stage for the stereotyped Other who, in the flashbacks, escapes what Janice Morgan identifies as the 'Western analysis or control'.[29] Morgan further shows that the separation between the white master and the racial and feminine stereotyped Other breaks political and cultural boundaries, which, in the case of *Chocolat*, she states are difficult to define. As for Gomes, it is possible to assert the same argument, as the relationship between Aurora and her husband practically only appears in scenes surrounding her lover, such as, for instance, in the outdoors party scene when Aurora looks attentively at Ventura, who is playing music at the party. The scenes almost exclude any emphasis on the husband, as she looks at her lover passionately while standing next to her husband. Thus, by making the relationship between the male gaze and the racialized Other almost non-existent, Denis and Gomes fragment the colonial fixity in a postcolonial discourse, which would otherwise subject them to being stereotyped. They subtly re-contextualize the male gaze to a non-controlling and quasi-powerless element through the construction of their characters' agency within colonial discourse.

By highlighting the existence and fixity of the stereotyped Other via flashbacks, Denis and Gomes both create a new type of post-colonial understanding. These directors illuminate and negotiate colonial and gender fixities that colonial discourses have imposed. As previously noted, both Bhabha and Mulvey explore in their theories the stereotyped Other and propagate, in different ways, this Other as excess in colonial discourse.

This article has argued that the two directors not only question the excess but also use the colonial to demonstrate how these fixities have been accepted as the social norm. The racial and feminine stereotyped Others represented in the films — France and Protée in *Chocolat* and Aurora, her servants, and Ventura in *Tabu* — may be considered on a par with other cultural productions, as representations that may not be seen or heard in any other way than as colonial excess. Nonetheless, by presenting these films through the direct viewpoint of France and of Ventura's mediation of Aurora's voice, the directors go beyond this norm of excess, and it is not by chance that these colonial stereotypes, to the audience, become owners of both their memories and their spatial mobility. Their silenced memories presented in the films and often expressed through their bodies, as referenced by France's burn and Aurora's death, are evidently subtle, difficult to see, and even more difficult to understand; however, the subtlety persists to show the continuous feeling of marginalization experienced by these women. In fact, to speak of the body is to use the body as a vehicle

---

[29] Janice Morgan, 'The Spatial Politics of Racial and Cultural Identity in Claire Denis' *Chocolat*', *Quarterly Review of Film and Video*, 20 (2003), 145–53 (p. 148).

for the memory and, more specifically, as a way to communicate the forgotten and the unseen. This is why, in turn, the directors' choices of camera angles become essential in defying theoretical truth claims, as these angles give the characters more personality and agency within post-colonial discourse, while still depicting different colonies and colonialisms.

In the end, the films' commonalities, like the feminine focus and the types of interactions between characters, allow for a comparison of the two distinct colonialisms. Both feminized memories almost force the spectator to view the films not only in a temporal, but also an ideological way; one that challenges claims that have silenced them. The movies make the audience confront taboos such as adultery or relationships that stood marginal to the white colonial order. The feminine focus and the feminine body allow each director to transmit the vision and transcend Bhabha's idea of fixity and subjectivity as well as Mulvey's male gaze. The flashbacks used in these movies, finally, demonstrate the need to question the livelihood and future of people, whose lived experiences have been portrayed in one official way in History. They show that there is a need to negotiate and analyse the untold lived experiences. Telling their stories to unfix their colonial identities and unsilence the memories in a way inscribes them in official history, for their fixity has virtually prevented their inscription in History in a way other than a painful memory. Additionally, these films question the relation of black people within the same discourse, as through those relationships one can learn about the powerful/privileged and the Other, or both.

Reviews

LUANA GIURGEVICH and HENRIQUE DE SOUSA LEITÃO, *Clavis Bibliothecarum: catálogos e inventários de livrarias de instituições religiosas em Portugal até 1834*, Fontes para o Estudo dos Bens Culturais da Igreja, 1 (Moscavide: Secretariado Nacional para os Bens Culturais da Igreja, 2016). 944 pages. Print.

Reviewed by JEREMY ROE (Faculdade de Ciências Sociais e Humanas — Universidade Nova de Lisboa — Centro de Humanidades)

Elaborating on the title of this work, the authors declare it to be 'uma chave para entrar no mundo imenso das antigas bibliotecas de mosteiros, conventos e instituições religiosas de Portugal' [a key to enter the vast world of the former libraries of Portuguese monasteries, convents and religious institutions]. It might be still better referred to as an immense bunch of keys to Portugal's diverse ecclesiastical libraries prior to the suppression of their respective religious institutions in 1834. The bulk of this book is a detailed catalogue of two corpora of archival documents relating to some 400 religious institutions. The first concerns 901 library catalogues and book inventories; the second 348 documents relating to these libraries. All these documents are methodically catalogued according to the diverse religious and military orders, as well as other devotional entities, to which they belonged, and their geographical locations. The meticulous structure of the book as a whole, as well the clarity of the individual entries, ensures its potential to fulfil the authors' aim to provide 'um instrumento' [an instrument] to develop 'a pesquisa a novas áreas e a horizontes explorados' [research in new areas and already explored horizons].

As might be expected, the majority of the documents from the first corpus of documents date from the eighteenth and nineteenth centuries, and above all circa 1834. Nonetheless, there are earlier documents to be traced. The lack of a chronological index of the documents catalogued in this book is felt at times, although the uncertain date of a number of the documents might have limited its value. The second corpus of documents contains a higher number of pre-eighteenth-century documents, such as Frei António de Araújo's catalogue of the library of the Mosteiro de Alcobaça, which also included a description of its decoration. This was later partially recorded in a drawing included in the 1701 manuscript catalogue *Aurea Clavis...*, illustrated in this book. A valuable collection of documents is listed for this royal library and illuminates its development and use. However, setting aside my own interests in Baroque cultural history, it must be underscored that this book provides a tool for a range of approaches to the history of libraries and books across the early modern and modern periods, as well as other related facets of ecclesiastical, cultural and intellectual history. Besides the catalogues of major libraries, such as the Alcobaça collection or Lisbon's Convent of Nossa Senhora de Jesus, which is today conserved in the Academia das Ciências de Lisboa, this book documents inventories of many more modest libraries, as well as individuals' personal collections in conjunction with diverse legal documents and correspondence that offer valuable perspectives on the histories of book collecting and reading in ecclesiastical libraries.

To orientate the reader's exploration of this monumental catalogue Giurgevich and Leitão provide a succinct introduction, which addresses the range and dimensions of ecclesiastical libraries over the course of their history up until 1834. They then focus on key facets of these libraries elucidated by the documents they catalogue, such as the control exerted over reading and the circulation of books. In addition to this a digital dimension to this book should also be highlighted. The book reviewed here is an independent and valuable resource in its own right, but the Biblioteca Nacional de Portugal also hosts a complementary website that provides access to digital editions of some of the documents catalogued: http://clavisbibliothecarum.bn.pt/index.php. While this site is still a work in progress, it provides readers with a valuable opportunity to begin exploring some of the many libraries to which *Clavis Bibliothecarum* offers a key.

Graciliano Ramos and the Making of Modern Brazil: Memories, Politics and Identities, ed. by SARA BRANDELLERO and LÚCIA VILLARES (Cardiff: University of Wales Press, 2017). 251 pages. Print and e-book.

Reviewed by PAUL MELO E CASTRO (University of Glasgow)

In the Anglophone world, Ramos's best-known novel *Vidas secas* has been read by several generations of students in the fields of Portuguese Studies and Comparative Literature and continues to be a staple of readings lists today. Yet a good deal of the criticism and commentary on Ramos's work in English dates back to the publication of Ralph E. Dimmick's 1963 translation, as *Barren Lives*, and is coloured by the atmosphere of the Cold War. It thus tends to dismiss or downplay Ramos's political affiliations and their influence on his writing, and to consider his novels in a narrowly regionalist context (as Darlene Sadlier has analysed in a fascinating article).[1] The publication of Brandellero and Villares's wide-ranging and nuanced volume, which both summarizes existing approaches and strikes out in new directions, thus provides a much-needed fillip to English-language scholarship and teaching on this canonical Brazilian author.

For those seeking an overview of Ramos's life and work, the volume provides good coverage of his background and career, in particular the political life of his natal state of Alagoas, in Randal Johnson's chapter, which offers a useful balance

[1] 'Reading Graciliano Ramos in the United States', *Luso-Brazilian Review*, 47.2 (2010), 1–25.

sheet of previous characterizations of Ramos's political opinions and narrates his political and literary life during his stint as Governor of Palmeira dos Índios and after the 1930 revolution. The volume then moves on to articles analysing the author's best-known works, focusing particularly, though not exclusively, on his four main novels *Caetés*, *São Bernardo*, *Vidas secas* and *Angústia*, along with *Infância*, Ramos's autobiographical account of his childhood years, and his prison memoir, *Memórias do cárcere*. All of these texts pick up and extend the 'psychoanalytic, Marxist and structuralist' approaches which have dominated scholarship on Ramos. Several of these articles are translations of research originally written (and in three cases, published) in Portuguese. One is from an Italian-language original. The volume thus provides a welcome opening up of Brazilian and international perspectives on Ramos's work for a monolingual English-language readership.

Of particular interest to scholars of Brazilian literature — and those concerned with how the Brazil that Ramos depicted led to the nation still attracting headlines for all the wrong reasons today — are the various proleptic connections made to later writers. These begin in the prefatory form of an interview with leading contemporary Brazilian novelist Luiz Ruffato and conclude with comparative readings of Ramos alongside authors as varied as Clarice Lispector, Silviano Santiago and Milton Hatoum. Eschewing some strands of Ramos scholarship which, as mentioned, tend to confine him to a regionalist framework, other articles delve the influence on his work of nineteenth century writers both in Portuguese (Eça de Queirós and Machado de Assis) and beyond (Flaubert, Dostoyevsky), and so reach out to those working both within and across national traditions of philology. In dealing with Ramos in the context of his contemporaries, the articles here consider the writer fully in his regionalist dimension but also as someone who wrote in the wake of global and Brazilian modernism and moved past any crudely social realist style. Indeed, as the volume's subtitle states, overall Ramos is analysed as a key writer on the experience of modernity in Brazil and as a figure of continued relevance today.

Given, as I mentioned at the outset, that the flow of English-language books on Ramos's work has rather dried up since the 1980s, *Graciliano Ramos and the Making of Modern Brazil* is a very welcome addition to scholarship. Even the recent turn to ecological concerns in criticism, which has given a new impetus to the study of canonical texts like *Vidas secas*, finds a thought-provoking comparator in Brandellero's article on Ramos's depiction of landscape. In short, instructors teaching Graciliano Ramos will find in this volume an instant bibliography whose individual components are very accessible to students. And researchers already familiar with Ramos's work will find the inspiration to return to his writing and find new perspectives for themselves.

ROBERTO VECCHI AND VINCENZO RUSSO, eds, *La letteratura portoghese: i testi e le idee* (Milan: Mondadori education, 2017). xv + 642 pages. Print.

Reviewed by SIMÃO VALENTE (Centre for Comparative Studies, University of Lisbon)

Roberto Vecchi and Vincenzo Russo's *La letteratura portoghese: i testi e le idee* will be the benchmark for Portuguese studies in Italy for years to come. It is an anthology of literary and critical texts covering the entire span of Portuguese literature, from its origins to the contemporary period. This type of book is especially relevant in a country where degrees and courses in literary and cultural studies tend to rely on anthologies and course books. What is particular to Vecchi and Russo's work, however, is the structure and presentation of the selected texts.

The book is divided into three parts, the first of which is titled 'From the Formation of Portugal to Empire', covering the years 1139 to 1580; the second section is called 'The Portuguese Empire and its Simulacra: From India to Brazil, and back', spanning the period from 1580 to 1851; the third and final part is 'The Splendour of Portugal and Beyond: From the Crisis of Constitutional Monarchy to Contemporary Portugal', which gathers texts from 1851 to 2016. Each of these parts is divided into chapters, which in turn contain the selected texts organized by author, each preceded by detailed biographical and critical notes introducing both the writers and their works. The three overarching parts include introductions that provide the necessary historical context to understand the texts that will follow. Similarly, a short conceptual synopsis concludes each of the parts, emphasizing the importance of empire in the formation of Portuguese culture. Bibliographical references and lists of Italian translations provide the reader with the information necessary to conduct further research.

One of the greatest merits of this anthology is that it will bring to Italian students of Portuguese a great variety of texts that would not otherwise be available. Many, if not most, of the selected excerpts in the first two parts are here published in Italy for the first time. This includes poetry, prose and theatre, but also essays and theory, up to the end of the nineteenth century. This is enriched by the fact that every single text is accompanied by an Italian translation, several of which were especially made for this volume.

Vecchi and Russo's critical introductions and synopses place Portuguese literature squarely in the theoretical framework of empire and its dissolution, and handle this issue with a level of nuance that takes into consideration the specificities of the Portuguese case as a semi-peripheral European nation, drawing mainly on the work of Eduardo Lourenço, Boaventura Sousa Santos and Margarida Calafate Ribeiro. This has been a fruitful strand in terms of advanced studies in Portuguese literature and culture for a few decades, but this anthology, by virtue of its introductory and didactic aim, frames a debate that has been so far at the cutting edge of research, as a point of departure for a new generation of readers.

Examples of how this is accomplished can also be gathered from analysing the selection, organization and presentation of texts. The second chapter of the third part is devoted to the *Geração de 70* [Generation of 1870]. It comprises seven texts, three by Eça de Queirós and the other four divided evenly between Antero de Quental and Oliveira Martins.[2] Of the three Eça texts, one is taken from *Os Maias* [The Maias]. It is a scene where João da Ega pinpoints the inconsistencies and shortcomings in European colonialism, lambasting with characteristic irony the professed good intentions in the name of progress by which economic exploitation takes place. This is certainly not a traditional take on Eça's novel, a book more commonly read for its treatment of the foibles of Portuguese bourgeoisie in line with French realism, particularly regarding love and marriage, with Carlos and Maria Eduarda's story taking centre stage. By choosing Ega's tirade as the anthologized piece, Russo and Vecchi are calling the reader's attention to underlying themes in Eça, and other authors, that may allow us to understand how they write about such things as love and marriage, but in the cultural context of empire.

As is often the case with anthologies, however, this deliberate choice made by the editors does at times leave out texts, authors and genres that do not entirely fit in with the organizing principle, in this case, empire. The book includes four texts by José Saramago, one of which is only available online, and five by António Lobo Antunes, thus favouring the latter as a representative of post-1974 Portuguese literature. Furthermore, all of Lobo Antunes's texts are related to the colonial wars and the Salazar regime. While those are certainly central topics in Antunes, his work goes beyond it. The same can be seen in the last chapter, devoted to the contemporary period. The title of this chapter is 'Post-memory Literature: *Post-everything* Portugal', and the selected authors are Isabela Figueiredo, Dulce Maria Cardoso, Lídia Jorge and Gonçalo M. Tavares. Tavares's text is an excerpt from *Viagem à Índia*, a piece that neatly illustrates the point Russo and Vecchi are making about Portuguese literature, but is also one of the few of Tavares's works that is more directly concerned with Portuguese history and literary tradition. A complete absence of post-1974 lyrical poetry also leaves out a large number of important writers — including some who started their careers in the 1950s or 60s — such as Nuno Júdice, Gastão Cruz, or Pedro Tamen, among others, whose works do not directly engage with Portuguese history, tending to have a more personal focus. This also applies to a younger generation of poets, those who started publishing in the 1990s, such as Ana Luísa Amaral or José Tolentino de Mendonça.

---

[2] One of the Oliveira Martins pieces is only available online, on the publisher's website, as is the case with several other texts in the volume. Nonetheless, the physical book includes them in its index and references them in the relevant part and chapter, directing the reader to the Internet. This is a practical and creative solution to the problems encountered by editors of anthologies.

That notwithstanding, when it comes to the first two parts of the anthology, Russo and Vecchi have managed to accomplish much more than gathering essential texts or those only pertaining to their central thesis. The fourth chapter of the first part is devoted to the *Cancioneiro Geral* [General Songbook] and chivalric prose, and the editors have opted to preserve the original spelling of the texts, a particularly commendable decision for a book that will help readers to get acquainted not only with Portugal's literature and history, but also the development of its language. In the second part there is also a chapter with texts by the sixteenth-century grammarians Fernão de Oliveira, João de Barros and Pêro Magalhães Gândavo, further tracing how Portuguese has changed over time. Chapters on Renaissance humanism and Baroque poetry and oratory also emphasize stylistic issues, while providing a useful framework to readers better acquainted with other European literatures, specifically Italian and Spanish.

To sum up, Russo and Vecchi's *La letteratura portoghese: i testi e le idee* is an invaluable resource for Italian-reading students of Portuguese, placing Portugal's literature in the historical context of empire while being mindful of the particularities of its case, namely the different roles of India, Brazil and Africa in the construction of the imperial myth. While this emphasis leaves out authors that are not directly concerned with writing about the national experience, the scope of the work as a university course book for those new to the history and language of Portugal underpins the editors' choices. The wealth of collected texts, critical notes and, crucially, translations available for the first time in Italy, is a welcome contribution to Portuguese studies.

Duarte I of Portugal, *The Book of Horsemanship*, trans. by JEFFREY L. FORGENG (Woodbridge, The Boydell Press, 2016). vii + 172 pages. Print and e-book.

Reviewed by STEPHEN PARKINSON (University of Oxford)

Relatively little of medieval Portuguese literature has made it into English translation, and prose has generally fared worse than poetry. The didactic works of the House of Aviz have remained particularly well hidden and need to be linked to specific topics to get noticed. This is the case with Dom Duarte's *Livro do cavalgar*, which has now been translated as part of a Boydell's *Armour and Weapons* series, to stand beside other medieval treatises on medieval warfare and chivalry.

Duarte's treatise continues a tradition initiated by his father Dom João I in his book of the hunt *Livro da Montaria*, but Duarte develops the theme in the systematic and reflective way which makes his better-known *Leal Conselheiro* such a personal work. Three chapters of the *Livro do cavalgar* were incorporated into the *Leal Conselheiro*, and the overall approach is on understanding, mental preparation and physical control, rather than on anatomy or technology. Forgeng appositely notes Duarte's deep interest in human understanding and motivation, in contrast to his sharing of the medieval view that the horse was a possession to be controlled rather than an intelligent being to be worked with.

The *Livro* is diligently classificatory, dividing each area into a number of distinct properties or qualities which are then systematically subclassified and itemized. Two short sections on Will (*voontade*) and Ability (*poder*) are followed by a longer treatment of Knowledge (*sabedoria*), which is the heart of the work and which remains incomplete, in that only seven of its sixteen categories are discussed. (Duarte seems to have interrupted the text after section 5 in 1433, the year of his accession, and completed two further sections when he resumed writing after a gap of four years.) The main categories of this property are Strength (*força*), Fearlessness (*seer sem receio*), Confidence (*segurança*), Firmness (*assessego*) and Fluidity (*soltura*). Firmness is developed in a detailed discussion of ways of avoiding falls, while *soltura* is key to jousting and hunting.

Forgeng uses the short title *Livro do cavalgar* which Duarte himself uses in references to it in *Leal Conselheiro*, and under which it is listed in the inventory of Duarte's library included in the *Livro dos Conselhos*. The full title *Livro da ensinança de bem cavalgar toda sela*, which appears at the beginning of the manuscript copy, is perhaps prematurely rejected on the grounds that it is not a title but a description. However, the translated title conserves the brevity of the short title while enriching it with the contents of the longer, and thus serves its purpose.

The translation reads well, which will make it accessible to its intended readership of students of medieval culture and the history of horses, horsemanship, and medieval martial arts. Forgeng is at great pains to establish and use the appropriate terminology for the elements of material culture involved, explaining them clearly in the extended introduction, and only using anachronism for intractable cases like *alveitaria* (translated as 'veterinary care' or 'veterinary medicine'). Other terms seem to be translated according to their drift rather than their connotations. The chapter on wrestling (which seems to have been outsourced, as Duarte introduces it as a text which he commissioned rather than composed) labels a whole series of manoeuvres as *erros*, which Forgeng translates as 'techniques', when 'moves' might have served better to respond to the gloss '*treta, ardil*' provided by the revered editor of the Portuguese text, Joseph Piel (who is curiously labelled a 'Lorrainian philologist'). The section on hunting refers to *animalias* as the broad group of beasts (including bears, bulls and boar) and *veaçom* for deer, all of which are translated as 'quarry'. The term *manha(s)*, which was Duarte's main term for the skills the knight needs to develop, and had not yet developed its modern connotations of slyness, comes out as the even more innocent-sounding 'art(s)'.

Forgeng is successful at simplifying the complexity of Duarte's prose without losing the flavour of the medieval treatise. He divides the text into short paragraphs according to the development of the description, rather than observing the division of the chapters by the pilcrow or *caldeirão* preserved in Piel's edition, and he remodels many phrases to achieve more direct and clearly structured discourse. This means jettisoning many of Duarte's favourite discourse connectors (*E, Ca, Pois*) and subordinating phrases such as *consiirando que, veendo que*, which weld the entire discussion into a single paragraph. Similarly, many sentences where the conditions or context precede the final conclusion are reversed and translated as simpler constructs in which a statement is followed by its explanation. Some of Duarte's many lists and enumerations are introduced by an editorial insertion such as 'in the following situations'. The account of wrestling moves makes wide use of the listing prefix *Item* widely found in wills and lists, which Forgeng for once translates literally as 'Item' when a formatted list might have been truer to the text. Forgeng modestly refrains from taking credit for his effort, by commenting on the directness of Duarte's style. At times the desire to simplify the syntax results in some loss of meaning (e.g. *fazer correger* translated as if it were plain *correger*), while in other cases a phrase is expanded (e.g. *todas cousas que fezer* as 'everything you have to do').

As Forgeng aptly notes, the text 'assumes a degree of prior technical knowledge of equestrianism', so that many activities and pieces of equipment are alluded to rather than described. Forgeng's informative and well organized introduction puts the work in its context and ably fills in these gaps, with sections on tack, jousting, riding and gaits, lanceplay, and sports. It has a few bibliographical and typographical blemishes (a pervasive misspelling *Conseilhero* in references to the *Leal Conselheiro*, references to Duarte's *Livro de Conselhos* as a treatise rather than a compilation, and one mention of its alternative title *Livro da Cartuxa* as a separate work).

The volume is elegantly produced and well illustrated, and will bring Duarte's treatise to a wider audience. Let us hope that the *Livro da Montaria* and other medieval guides will follow in its footsteps.

MARIA ADELAIDE MIRANDA and ALICIA MIGUÉLEZ CAVERO, eds, *Portuguese Studies on Medieval Illuminated Manuscripts* (Barcelona and Madrid: Fédération Internationale des Instituts d'Études Médiévales, 2014). xvi + 196 pages, 8 black and white illustrations, 28 colour illustrations, 3 tables. Print and e-book.

Reviewed by ANDRÉ B. PENAFIEL (University of Oxford)

Portuguese Studies on Medieval Illuminated Manuscripts presents the reader with eight articles written in English and French, some of which were originally presented at the Fifth Congress of the Fédération Internationale des Instituts d'Études Médiévales, held in June 2013, in Porto. The articles are dedicated to a variety of manuscripts, which range from the twelfth to the fifteenth century and are predominantly in Latin, with a few exceptions (Lusitanists should note that none of them are in the Portuguese language). There are manuscripts of both Portuguese and non-Portuguese origin, and they are held in collections both in Portugal and abroad. Thus, *Portuguese Studies* in the title does not relate to the subject matter, but to the fact that the authors of this volume are based at Portuguese universities, namely the Universidade Nova de Lisboa and Universidade de Lisboa. Overall, this book showcases the complementary approaches of work currently undertaken in these two institutions in the areas of art history, conservation and codicology. The readership of this book is therefore broad and, while relevant for Lusitanists, it is certainly not restricted to them.

In the first article, the reader will find a study by Maria Adelaide Miranda and Maria João Melo on the use of colour pigments in twelfth- and thirteenth-century manuscripts produced by three Portuguese monasteries: São Mamede do Lorvão, Santa Maria de Alcobaça and Santa Cruz de Coimbra. The authors analyse a total of thirty-eight manuscripts, a sample of the surviving holdings currently in three Portuguese public libraries, Arquivos Nacionais da Torre do Tombo, Biblioteca Pública Municipal do Porto and Biblioteca Nacional de Portugal. The material analysis of pigments allows them to detect the origin of the substances used by the scriptoria, and whether these were expensive or required any special technical skill. The authors claim to have developed a new methodology called 'colour mapping': they calculate the colours used in a manuscript or a collection and offer a pie chart representing how each colour has been used proportionately in the samples from each monastery and in a particular manuscript. There is also a very brief case study of a specific manuscript, the *Apocalypse of Lorvão* (shelfmark: Torre do Tombo, Ordem de Cister, Mosteiro de Lorvão, códice 44), which is a copy of the *Commentary on the Apocalypse* by Beatus of Liébana.

Rita Castro, Melo and Miranda write on *De avibus*, by Hugh of Fouilloy, a twelfth-century moralized treatise on birds. They focus on three Portuguese manuscripts from the monasteries of Lorvão, Santa Cruz de Coimbra and Alcobaça (shelfmarks: Lorvão 5, DGARQ-ANTT; Ms. 34 Santa Cruz, BPMP; ALC 238, BNP). According to their proposed dating, all three manuscripts are from the late twelfth century. In this article, the authors begin with a larger European perspective, highlighting the importance of the Portuguese copies specifically. Based on the manuscripts' iconography, they establish a broad genealogical relationship between manuscripts, arguing that the three Portuguese examples and a French manuscript from Clairvaux abbey (shelfmark: Ms. 177, Bibliothèque Municipale de Troyes) can be divided into two main groups. In the vein of the previous study, they document pigments used in the Portuguese manuscripts and employ the colour mapping technique for their analysis. In a final section, they point out that Hugh of Fouilloy interprets symbolically the colours of birds (e.g. the dove's white colour represents divine grace) and the authors explore how illuminators based their own depiction of birds on the text.

Alicia Cavero investigates a map in the twelfth-century *Apocalypse of Lorvão* manuscript (shelfmark: Torre do Tombo, Ordem de Cister, Mosteiro de Lorvão, códice 44). She begins by contextualizing how this map relates to other extant copies. Cavero then describes the map, of which only half survives and raises hypotheses about its history, including how it was created independently from the rest of the manuscript and how it was detached from the bound codex. From a survey of nineteenth- and twentieth-century literature, she then documents how it was inserted on two separate occasions into the codex. There is a range of codicological observations, from which the author derives her conclusions.

Maria Alessandra Bilotta studies a fourteenth-century glossed copy of the *Decretals* of Gregory IX, a legal text by Raymond de Peñafort. The manuscript, of French origin, is currently at the Torre do Tombo (shelfmark: Ordem de São Jerónimo, Mosteiro de Santa Maria de Belém, liv. 81). Bilotta offers a general description of the manuscript, including palaeography, page layout, marginalia and the interpolation of later texts (specifically the *Novellae* of Innocent IV). She proceeds to a more detailed study of the five illuminations in the manuscript, which she identifies as the work of a French illuminator who also worked on two manuscripts currently in Reims. She reproduces and describes these illuminations, explaining how they are linked to the text. Bilotta also argues that the production of this manuscript reveals collaboration between southern and northern France, with a scribe and the illuminator possibly based in Paris, a second scribe of southern origin and the book itself dedicated to members of the University of Toulouse.

Catarina Barreira discusses a specific manuscript of the *Compendium theologicae veritatis*, by Hugh Ripelin of Strasburg, a thirteenth-century theological text which was extensively copied and printed until the sixteenth century. The manuscript (shelfmark: Biblioteca Nacional de Portugal, Alc. 376) comes from Alcobaça abbey's scriptorium and the author outlines the importance of the abbey's library and its links with Clairvaux Abbey. She focuses on the eight historiated initials of this manuscript which are described, analysed and occasionally reproduced. She analyses the similarities between the initials in this manuscript and those found in another from the same scriptorium (shelfmark: Alc. 26). Finally, the author argues that historiated initials were rare in manuscripts from this scriptorium.

Luís Ribeiro is interested in the iconographic representation of the artist in the fifteenth century. He offers an overview of astrology in the Middle Ages, why each planet came to symbolize certain ideas, and how the planets became associated with certain trades or social roles. He describes the iconographic representation of Mercury in a German manuscript (shelfmark: Tübingen, Universitätsbibliothek, Md 2), an English manuscript (shelfmark: Bodleian Ms. Rawl. D. 1220) and a clock-face painting. Ribeiro also explores how the ideas associated with Mercury and Venus could overlap, in particular as different artists or artistic crafts could be associated with either of those planets.

Ana Lemos, Rita Araújo, Conceição Casanova, Melo and Vânia Muralha focus on two French-style books of hours from the fifteenth century (shelfmarks:

Biblioteca Nacional de Portugal, IL. 15 and IL. 19). They describe the pigments used in the illuminations of both manuscripts according to their molecular composition and preparation. The analysis relies on at least two techniques, microspectrofluorimetry and Raman spectroscopy. The authors conclude that, although the illuminations in these two manuscripts look similar in terms of colour, the inks used were significantly different, leading them to propose that IL. 15 is from a Flemish workshop, whereas IL. 19 is French. Furthermore, they propose that folio 84 of IL. 15 was originally located between folios 98 and 99 of IL. 19. The deduction is based on a variety of arguments, including an analysis of the binding structure, the comparison of the style of the illuminations, the identification of a textual lacuna in IL. 19 and the analysis of the pigments.

Finally, Luís Afonso and Tiago Moita study twenty-six Portuguese Hebrew illuminated manuscripts, mostly religious in content, currently scattered across different libraries and dating from the late fifteenth century. The authors divide the manuscripts into four groups based on an analysis of the illuminated frames which occupy the leaf margins. They contrast the Portuguese Hebrew style with that found in manuscripts from Andalusia and Toledo. In their analysis, they suggest that the Portuguese manuscripts were influenced by Italian illumination, both Hebrew and Christian, specifically by books from Ferrara, Florence and Naples. They conclude that the style of the illuminations found in the Portuguese Hebrew manuscripts studied reveals a synthesis of Hebrew and Christian art, including influences of Gothic and Renaissance styles. They contrast this with Andalusian Hebrew manuscripts which, in turn, would be closer to an Islamic style.

The book has a preface by Patricia Stirneman, an introduction by Cavero and closes with two indices. Overall, the reader finds in this volume collaborative research between art historians and conservators, and the development of material analysis applied to a variety of manuscripts.

GEORGE MONTEIRO, *There's No Word for 'Saudade': Perspectives on the Literature and Culture of Portuguese America* (New York: Peter Lang, 2017). 218 pages. Print and e-book.

GEORGE MONTEIRO, *Caldo Verde is Not Stone Soup: Persons, Names, Words, and Proverbs in Portuguese America* (New York: Peter Lang, 2017). 254 pages. Print and e-book.

Reviewed by CARMEN RAMOS VILLAR (University of Sheffield)

For those of us who research on Portuguese American literature, George Monteiro is a very familiar name. He has written very insightful introductions to Portuguese American works, as well as essays which explore Portuguese American literature. He is also a good poet. It would be wrong, however, to think that Monteiro's work is solely directed at those who are interested in all things Portuguese American. A good example of his versatility is this latest compilation of essays, which compose volumes 4 and 5 of Peter Lang's Interdisciplinary Studies in Diasporas series. These two volumes bring together some of Monteiro's writings on the Portuguese American community and on a diverse range of subjects, from proverbs and nicknames to the reception of translations on both sides of the Atlantic. Roughly divided, volume 4 looks at literature and literary production and volume 5 examines more traditional, popular knowledge.

The spirit in both volumes is one of an exchange of observations, a conversation in which Monteiro shares with the reader his joy at finding things out and making connections. See, for instance, the essay on the reception of the translation of two nineteenth-century Portuguese novels by Eça de Queirós and Júlio Dinis in volume 4, where Monteiro helpfully traces how the nineteenth-century American public received them, and also the authors' reactions to how their work was reshaped and changed to suit the new readership. Another example, also in the same volume, is the essay on the life of John Francis, a second-generation Portuguese American who became something like a patron of the arts and a go-between for the group of American writers known as 'The Players'. In this essay, Monteiro explores a seemingly insignificant, perhaps forgotten, person, slowly building a picture with other essays within the volume that touch upon John Francis, so as to provide a surprising piece of social history. In so doing, Monteiro fleshes out the wider representation and portrayal of the Portuguese in the US, something of a running theme in most of the essays in this volume. Singling out another essay within volume 4, entitled '"Old Country" Movies', Monteiro provides another example of reading about social history at the same time as he explores several iconic Portuguese films of the 1940s. He starts by describing how these films were viewed by the Portuguese American community in the New Bedford of his childhood, and then explains how seeing them 'some fifty years later, under the auspices of the Portuguese Cultural Foundation, directed by Regina Emerson' (p. 168) changed his perception and triggered the essay. The result is a careful close reading which highlights the theme of imprisonment that permeates these films, showing his surprise at how such criticism of the Estado Novo escaped the censors at the time.

Still on volume 4, for those interested in Portuguese American literature, there are a number of essays that deserve careful reading. To begin with, two essays provide an overview of both American and Portuguese American authors ('Poems, Persons, and Things' and 'Fiction Writers'), which not only showcase Monteiro's usual sharp and sensitive critical eye, but also provide new Portuguese American names listed and analysed that are not included in existing survey articles about Portuguese American literature — and some of them are women authors. In a similar vein, the last essay, 'No Word for *Saudade*', treads a familiar path of examining famous American authors who are scathing in their portrayals of the Portuguese, but Monteiro nevertheless provides really interesting insights in his examination of them. The essay on Olívio Lopes and Thomas Braga, for instance, taps into a similar approach seen in the essays about John dos Passos and John Philip Sousa within this volume: how an author deals with the Portuguese American experience by either embracing it fully, or distancing himself from it. The essays on Onésimo Teotónio Almeida, Frank X. Gaspar, Julian Silva and Charles Reis Felix are sensitive close readings that situate the author in question within the community they write from, something which allows Monteiro to scrutinize their work insightfully. As always, Monteiro's observations also leave room for others to take the analysis further if they wish. Each essay in volume 4, then, provides a different perspective that advances the understanding of the works under Monteiro's gaze, becoming a good source of information for researchers in this field as well as the general reader.

In Volume 5, Monteiro could be said to showcase his enjoyment for learning, and for sharing knowledge. This time, the subject matter is popular culture: nicknames and how these were transplanted and changed by the Portuguese in the US; collecting Portuguese proverbs in the US, sometimes by trawling through the printed press or by conducting oral history projects; and even demonstrating how stories become myths, and larger-than-life tales at the service of certain social and political discourses, such as when he examines the life of Peter Francisco. Of note, the essay entitled 'Authenticity and its Uses' is an educating and entertaining read where Monteiro writes about his own interpretation of what Rodrigues Miguéis wrote on the margin of Pires de Lima's *adagiário* when he read it. This essay, a reading of someone else's reading, not only provides a window into the mind of Rodrigues Miguéis, but also gives useful hints and tips on how to organize and categorize a collection of proverbs (which Monteiro will later put into practice in the same volume). It is also quite a funny read. For those interested in Portuguese American culture, the essays in Part I, Part II and Part V in volume 5 are an interesting mixture of subjects to dip into, touching upon social history, *crónica*, academic study, and a recording of instances and mentions of early Portuguese American people in the printed press. For instance, the essay 'Denizens in the Land of Nod' reproduces the obituaries of early Portuguese emigrants to the US, and is a window onto the society these people lived in at the time. Another example is the essay which traces the word 'gee' (i.e. Portuguese) from its origin up to the time it became a term of derision. The last essay in volume 5, 'Henry R. Lang on the Portuguese in New Bedford', looks sympathetically at the folklore and social customs at the turn of the nineteenth and twentieth centuries, providing a snapshot of the community at the time. On the other hand, the essay '150 Years of a Classic' traces the origins of Pedro Carolino's disastrous manual of English conversation for Portuguese speakers, and explains how the text became an instant classic with American readers, for all the wrong reasons. Bearing in mind some of the essays from volume 4 dealing with how authors depicted the Portuguese emigrant in the US, what Monteiro incrementally shows is the construction of a specific image of the Portuguese that gradually crystalized over time.

Although there is an element of repetition, sometimes of whole sentences and paragraphs, the two volumes are worth dipping into for the insightful examinations on American, Portuguese American and Portuguese works. They are also highly entertaining essays in themselves, which show just how much fun Monteiro had with writing them in the first place, and how much he enjoys sharing his knowledge.

Abstracts

Irony in the 'Peregrinação'
THOMAS EARLE

ABSTRACT. The first part of the article is a review of some of the principal critical writings about Mendes Pinto's famous book, from the seventeenth century to the twentieth, drawing attention to the important but forgotten work of the nineteenth-century scholar, José Feliciano de Castilho. In the second part there is an attempt to reconcile the contradictions of the critical tradition by a reading which emphasizes the rhetorical use of irony in the *Peregrinação*, both verbal and situational. Mendes Pinto's ironical attitude to man and his works is undercut by his faith in divine Providence.
KEYWORDS. Mendes Pinto, *Peregrinação*, irony, Francis Xavier, Japan, travel.

RESUMO. Nas primeiras páginas do artigo passam-se em revista alguns dos mais significativos juízos críticos acerca do conhecido livro de Mendes Pinto, desde o século XVII até ao século XX, chamando-se a atenção ao trabalho importante, mas esquecido, do investigador novecentista José Feliciano de Castilho. Na segunda parte tenta-se reconciliar as contradições da tradição crítica, através de uma leitura que salienta a retórica irónica, verbal e situacional encontrada na *Peregrinação*. Mesmo assim, a atitude irónica de Mendes Pinto para com o homem e os feitos humanos fica desmentida pela sua fé na Providência Divina.
PALAVRAS-CHAVE. Mendes Pinto, *Peregrinação*, ironia, S. Francisco Xavier, Japão, viagens.

Geographical Knowledge and Mineral Riches in the Struggle for Sovereignty and Possession of Southern Brazil (1750–1755)
DENISE MOURA

ABSTRACT. The construction of Portuguese sovereignty on the lands of southern Brazil in the eighteenth century triggered a dispute between the Portuguese Crown and the sertanistas (backwoodsmen), who both supported their arguments for rights to the lands with documents, such as manuscripts and maps, which confirmed that they had geographical knowledge of the area. The starting point of this dispute was when a geographer from Genoa, Francesco Tosi Colombina, was hired by the Portuguese Crown to write a manuscript plan to explore the Sertões do Tibagi in 1752, whose repercussion was to prompt the sertanista Angelo Pedroso to order a map of the same lands and put in question the Italian-sertanista cartography.
KEYWORDS. State, sovereignty, rights of states, boundaries, territorial rights,

geography, cartography, maps, geographers, geographical exploration, mineral resources, southern Brazil, wilderness.

Resumo. A construção da soberania portuguesa nas terras do Brasil meridional no século XVIII provocou disputas entre a Coroa portuguesa e sertanistas, que sustentaram seus argumentos de direitos sobre terras com manuscritos e mapas que confirmavam seus conhecimentos geográficos. O ponto inicial desta disputa ocorreu quando um geógrafo de Gênova, Francesco Tosi Colombina, foi contratado pela Coroa portuguesa em 1752 para escrever um plano de exploração dos sertões do Tibagi cuja repercussão foi levar o sertanista Angelo Pedroso a encomendar um mapa das mesmas terras e questionar a cartografia ítalo-sertanista.

Palavras-chave. Estado, soberania, direitos, direitos de estado, limites, direitos territoriais, geografia, cartografia, geógrafos, exploração geográfica, recursos minerais, Brasil meridional, sertões.

Transnational Perspectives in Early Twentieth-Century Portugal: The Emergence of the Periodical 'Sociedade Futura' (Lisbon, 1902–1904)
Christina Bezari

Abstract. This article explores the representations of foreign cultures and literatures in the Portuguese periodical *Sociedade Futura* (Lisbon, 1902–1904). Special attention is given to the concept of transnationality, which occupied a prominent place in the writings of Ana de Castro Osório and Maria Sarmento da Silveira. By drawing on a range of rare publications and historical sources, this study explains how the two editors incorporated foreign influences in their periodical in order to reassert the norms of their native culture and reinforce the need for social change. A transnational approach to editorship will provide a firm ground for the study of women's contribution to public debate and their role in shaping society and culture.

Keywords. *Sociedade Futura*, female editors, transnational, press, early twentieth century, Ana de Castro Osório, Maria Sarmento da Silveira.

Resumo. Este artigo explora as representações de culturas e literaturas estrangeiras na revista portuguesa *Sociedade Futura* (Lisboa, 1902–1904). Demos especial atenção ao conceito de transnacionalidade, que ocupou um lugar central nos escritos de Ana de Castro Osório e Maria Sarmento da Silveira. A partir de um conjunto de publicações e fontes históricas escassas, este estudo explica como as duas editoras incorporaram influências estrangeiras no seu periódico, a fim de reafirmar as normas da sua cultura nativa e reforçar a necessidade de mudança social. Uma abordagem transnacional da editoração constituirá uma base sólida para o estudo da contribuição das mulheres para o debate público e do seu papel na formação da sociedade e da cultura.

Palavras-chave. *Sociedade Futura*, mulheres editoras, transnacional, imprensa, início do século XX, Ana de Castro Osório, Maria Sarmento da Silveira.

Hybridity and Prejudice: Jews and New Christians in 'Casa-Grande & Senzala' and the Intellectual Context of Gilberto Freyre
CLAUDE B. STUCZYNSKI

ABSTRACT. The question of Gilberto Freyre's anti-Jewish proclivities is a matter generally omitted by most of scholars, since his views on colonial Brazil celebrated human miscegenation and cultural *métissage* as quintessential to Brazil's identity. How could a champion of Brazil's 'racial democracy' and a pioneer of historiographical hybridism, like Freyre, express anti-Semitic stereotypes imbued with racialist overtones? This article aims to give some answers to this riddle through a textual and contextual analysis of Freyre's masterpiece: *Masters and Slaves (Casa Grande & Senzala*, 1933). After reviewing past scholarship on this issue (mostly related to his education and early biography), I will first show the influence of the Portuguese-Brazilian historian João Lúcio de Azevedo on Freyre's views on Jews, conversos and Judaism. On the other hand, I will argue that Freyre's reification of 'the Jew' paradoxically comes from his way of depicting Brazil's identity as an inclusive combination between different 'races', cultures and 'characters'. A comparison with Américo Castro's narratives of Spain, as stemming from an interaction between Christians, Muslims and Jews, will show that Freyre's anti-Jewish prejudices paradoxically emerged from his 'mestizo' views.
KEYWORDS. Hybridism, anti-Semitism, racism, historiography, national identity, Jews, New Christians (conversos), João Lúcio de Azevedo, Américo Castro, Franz Boas, Gilberto Freyre, *Casa-Grande & Senzala*.

RESUMO. A questão das tendências anti-semitas de Gilberto Freyre é um assunto geralmente omitido pela maioria dos estudiosos, uma vez que suas visões sobre o Brasil colonial celebravam a miscigenação humana e a mestiçagem cultural como essencial para a identidade do Brasil. Como poderia um defensor da 'democracia racial' do Brasil e um pioneiro do hibridismo historiográfico, como Freyre, expressar estereótipos anti-semitas imbuídos de conotações racistas? Este artigo pretende dar algumas respostas a este enigma através de uma análise textual e contextual da obra-prima de Freyre: *Casa Grande & Senzala* (1933). Depois de passar em revista estudos anteriores sobre esta questão (principalmente relacionados à sua educação e biografia), mostrarei primeiramente a influência do historiador luso-brasileiro João Lúcio de Azevedo nas visões de Freyre sobre os judeus, os conversos e o judaísmo. Por outro lado, argumentarei que a reificação de Freyre do 'judeu' vem paradoxalmente de sua maneira de descrever a identidade do Brasil como uma combinação inclusiva entre diferentes 'raças', culturas e 'personagens'. Uma comparação com as narrativas de Américo Castro sobre a Espanha, como decorrente de uma interação entre cristãos, muçulmanos e judeus, mostrará que os preconceitos antijudaicos de Freyre emergiram paradoxalmente de suas visões 'mestiças'.

PALAVRAS-CHAVE. Hibridismo, anti-semitismo, racismo, historiografia, identidade nacional, Judeus, Cristãos-novos (conversos), João Lúcio de Azevedo, Américo Castro, Franz Boas, Gilberto Freyre, *Casa-Grande & Senzala*.

Pessoa, Unknown to Paz
JERÓNIMO PIZARRO

ABSTRACT. 'El desconocido de sí mismo' [A Stranger to Himself], the foreword that Octavio Paz wrote almost sixty years ago for his anthology of Fernando Pessoa, is still today one of the best introductions to Pessoa's poetry. The purpose of this article is to study the sources of the essay written by Paz, which was important not only because it introduced Pessoa's poetry to the Hispanic world, but also because it was a source for a broader understanding of the history of modern poetry for Paz himself, given that when he wrote *El arco y la lira* [The Bow and the Lyre] (1956) he had a limited knowledge of Portuguese literature and he did not yet know Pessoa. Outstanding among the sources of the essay is one in which Pessoa himself, answering the request of a friend, refers his literary influences between 1904 and 1913. The final considerations defend the need for a better understanding and knowledge of Portuguese literature — and other less read and studied literatures — to 'decentralize' our knowledge of some literary traditions.
KEYWORDS. Octavio Paz, Fernando Pessoa, 'A Stranger to Himself', literary influences, modern poetry, Portuguese literature.

RESUMO. 'El desconocido de sí mismo' [O desconhecido de si mesmo], o prefácio que Octavio Paz escreveu há quase sessenta anos para a sua antologia de Fernando Pessoa, é, ainda hoje, uma das melhores introduções à poesia pessoana. O propósito deste artigo é estudar as fontes do prefácio-ensaio de Paz, que foi importante tanto para a divulgação hispânica de Pessoa como para um entendimento mais alargado da história da poesia moderna por parte de Paz, sendo que o poeta mexicano, quando escreveu *El arco y la lira* [O arco e a lira] (1956), ainda não conhecia Pessoa e sabia pouco da literatura portuguesa. Das fontes do prefácio, destaca-se uma em que o próprio Pessoa indica, a pedido de um escritor amigo, quais foram, entre 1904 e 1913, as suas influências literárias. Nas considerações finais, defende-se a necessidade de conhecer melhor a literatura escrita em português — tal como outras literaturas menos lidas e estudadas — para 'descentralizar' o nosso conhecimento de algumas tradições literárias.
PALAVRAS-CHAVE. Octavio Paz, Fernando Pessoa, 'O desconhecido de si mesmo', influências literárias, poesia moderna, literatura portuguesa.

Fragmenting Colonial Stereotypes in the Films 'Chocolat' (1988) and 'Tabu' (2012)
SANDRA RELLIER

ABSTRACT. This article draws on elements of postcolonial and feminist theory to raise the question of 'whose post-colonial?' and examines the norm of excess, which condemns the silenced Other. By analysing how the films *Chocolat* (1988) and *Tabu* (2012) fragment the fixity of the colonial gaze in relation to the black Other and woman as Other, this study revisits Homi Bhabha's idea of the fixed colonial stereotype and Laura Mulvey's concept of the male gaze. Further, the analysis calls attention to how both films embrace the technique of the flashback that both challenges the problematic of the 'colonized Other' and negotiates colonial memories in colonial/post-colonial discourses.
KEYWORDS. Male gaze, colonial gaze, postcolonialism, Bhabha, Mulvey, *Chocolat*, *Tabu*.

RESUMO. Este artigo usa pressupostos da teoria pós-colonial e da teoria feminista para questionar a pertença do pós-colonial e examina a norma do excesso que condena o Outro silenciado. Ao analisar como os filmes *Chocolat* (1988) e *Tabu* (2012) fragmentam a rigidez do olhar colonial em relação ao Outro negro e ao Outro feminino, este estudo revisita a ideia do estereótipo colonial de Homi Bhabha e o conceito do olhar masculino de Laura Mulvey. Além disso, a análise chama a atenção como ambos os filmes adotam a técnica do flashback que desafia a problemática do outro colonial e que negocia as memórias coloniais nos discursos coloniais/pós-coloniais.
PALAVRAS-CHAVE. Olhar masculino, olhar colonial, pós-colonialismo, Bhabha, Mulvey, *Chocolat*, *Tabu*.

www.ingramcontent.com/pod-product-compliance
Lightning Source LLC
Chambersburg PA
CBHW071407290426
44108CB00014B/1718